THE MANMADE WILDERNESS

CLARA W. MAYER

THE

MANMADE
WILDERNESS

NEW YORK

ATHENEUM
1964

To Bernhard and Sophia Mayer,

who knew their destination and

kept the way clear.

AUTHOR'S NOTE

This small volume is born of a great purpose and a greater faith, yet its immediate aims are modest.

Out of an elemental urge toward clarity in a bewildered and bewildering world, it seeks to discover whether an inner compulsion is sweeping us irresistibly to our doom. Or whether the simple human virtues, simply and singly cultivated—not by mass communication or other mass methods—can cut through the mountains of confusion, restore in each of us the sense of confidence and purpose, and so in the nation and the world. For this one seeker the answer is positive.

Other than that, its intent is not to exhaust thought on any subject but to stimulate thought. The form, for the most part, is general, philosophical—as the touchstone of validity—sometimes with examples; but, stated or unstated, the source of the generalization is always a specific situation, the need to penetrate its complications, to understand and follow its component forces.

Portions of these chapters have appeared in the *Bulletin of the New School for Social Research.*

Spring, 1958

PREFACE

Predominating in each of us is the individual or the social being. The individual prompted the Author's Note, written earlier than this preface, the hope, in the initial stages of thinking and writing, that the problems of humanity might be solved in individual terms, with multiple individual efforts.

But it has become clear that such efforts would be too much to expect in the light of the existing industrial atomization and conformity that have begun to calcify the impulses toward individuality and responsibility with their very limited use to the industrial machine. Moreover, it would be to ignore the forces that have produced social constructs and cohesion from coral to clans, from insect communities to cities and states. But the insect communities have this difference: with their apparently immutable functional castes, they are more or less stable; the element of long-range social ambition in human communities, with its complement of social protest, therefore of shifting emancipation and exploitation, makes for corresponding periods of exaltation, of social frustration and deterioration. These latter tend toward a desperation that may be enhanced by technical and other primary and secondary changes only partially subsumed under "cultural lag"—shorthand for the jagged thrusts forward and back, upward and down, evident in the most random attempt at a graphic portrayal of our culture.

For society in a sense makes us over, each in his kind. Prestige, which has only social meaning, is for one man to amass wealth endlessly, unconverted to private or public use, eternally potential. For another, prestige is to collect board memberships, business or philanthropic, which have no real counterpart, whether in genuine interest, in responsibility or knowledge. For a third, it is his art collection or his library, of which the primary appeal is neither artistic nor literary but fashionable. And without society there is no fashion— just one example of the perversions that human nature is heir to in society, notwithstanding "it is born in fellowship and decays in isolation."

The suppressed cry that runs through these pages is for livable life: for the opportunity to enjoy the wealth and the beauty we have inherited and to a degree created, by taking the responsibility of choice, by recognizing in consumption as in performance that the complement of choosing is the readiness to forgo, that in the survival of the human race as of the human individual, "fortune favors the brave" and the resolute.

Spring, 1963

CONTENTS

THE MANMADE WILDERNESS

CHAPTER

1

PERSONALITY

Civilized Values Depend on Each Man Being

Himself, and

Being Content to Express the Best that He

Believes to Be in Him

The London Times had this to say when Max Beerbohm died: "Personality is easier to recognize than to define. . . . There was a timeless quality about him that made mock of the passing of the generations. He did not date because the unique integrity of his outlook on the human comedy was dateless. . . . His individualism, maintained so modestly, yet with such unshakable resolution, was a reminder that civilized values depend on each man being himself and being content to express the best that he believes to be in him."

Is it becoming more and more difficult for each man to be himself? Especially in America; and if it is, why is it? Do competitive sports, on which we pride ourselves, contribute to greater difficulty? Does competitive business, free enterprise, on which again we pride ourselves, however few of those in it are any longer free? Do competitive schools contribute? Have we, in short, created a competitive society in which we lack criteria except to best the other fellow? A lack carried finally into international policy, even outer space.

This lack of criteria supervenes upon a state of mind that appears to have led, by imperceptible stages, from the spirit of independence of the pioneer to the need for power of the bureaucrat at every level—power to assure and to reassure him that he is still a man—from the clerk to the president, with prerogatives and duties job defined in petty gradations of power which the corporate structure makes sacred.

The late Robert Frost identified as a principal activity of these days trying to find and "to put back" things we have lost in the course of what we used to call progress—as we put vitamins back into bread. The current assignment is to put personality, individuality, back into life. It is an all but impossible task, because our social and economic institutions, small scale or large, are breeding not for personality but for what they conceive to be mass appeal and efficiency, that same "efficiency" that shows signs of breaking down on every hand. We are left with the organization man, who begins to look universal, found not only where we expect to find him but equally where we do not; power struggle, chain of command, buck passing haunt every organization. They are in no way confined to the marketplace or the military.

To have power need not mean to exercise it, as witness the extreme case of the Nazarene. This is the difference between power and leadership. And genuine love of freedom asserts itself not primarily in protest against abuse of power by others, but in fundamental alienation from any show of power, especially one's own.

In the day's vernacular one asks, "Where do we go from here?"; where indeed must we go? And the only reply we can make, if we wish to escape our own tyranny, is to rediscover personality, to know the joy born of genuine independence and its inevitable reciprocal, joy in the independence of others, in each man's being himself, until his individualism, "maintained modestly yet with unshakable resolution," brings home to him "that civilized values depend on it and on his being content to express the best that he believes to be in him."

Alas "the times are out of joint"; the Max Beerbohms few and disappearing. A crushing illusion of helplessness persuades us of the futility even of the best we believe to be in us. The quantitative in life has overwhelmed the qualitative.

Personality, individuality, creativity, have become smothering clichés of the sparks that ignited them. With activities programs, projects, and "research" that begins at the age of seven—fifty requests for books on Chinese religion from second graders, on a single day in the children's division of the Forty-second Street Library!—with such a travesty of what was meant to be education for originality and independent thinking, even the children have forged their iron conventions.

Not the voice of the people but the voice of TV and radio has become the voice of God—can one say more of anything than that it is a nationally advertised brand? And mass communication is not mass communication, we are told by one learned foundation official, but "communication with individuals by a mass method."

The role of education, as we conceive it, is to make actual what is potential in a given personality. Learning and teaching are essentially individual, in method and in aim: to self-development there is neither short cut nor assembly line. In the long run profoundly satisfying, it remains none the less an unremitting effort for discrimination, perspective, keen insights, clear values. If we are lucky, it goes on to the end of life and, at the close, the game proves worth the candle.

For the joy of life or its haplessness is basically a matter of attitude, and the resulting ability or inability to make the most of it—not what, but how we experience determines whether, spiritually, we accumulate capital or debt.

"Possibly more potent than destiny," writes a German poet, "is the unfaltering courage to bear it"; in our version, the positive courage to meet it. From insignificant to major, from disastrous to triumphant, from experience of poverty or of wealth, short of destruction itself, the human spirit has the capacity to rise to experience and develop, or to be leveled by it and succumb. Between such extremes of misery and magnificence range the varieties of the human individual.

This is a thesis as easily examined in life as in history, even in the inorganic world; the strength of an electric current depends on the resistance it overcomes, and greatness is inextricably linked with the obstacles it surmounts. In science the genius is measured by the basic significance of the problems he "discovers" and solves or, it may be, fails to solve. The part of statesmen is to distill the wisdom of history, with it to undermine the towering mass of man's stupidities; of such we speak as men of the hour.

And we revert to the eternal dilemma: does the man make the hour, the hour the man, or both an indissoluble unit? In the longer, larger vistas of space and time, is it providence or chance we discern, fate or circumstance, determinism or free will, instrumentality or hero?

Answers are individual and personal, in terms of courage, self-confidence, resolution and faith. Independent of one another, these have the single common characteristic that each may increase or diminish its power according to how, as personalities, we respond to experience: challenged, enriched, bowled over, or uninfluenced by its limitless potential.

Both pleasure and suffering crystallized St. Francis' humanity. For Franklin Roosevelt paralysis became decisively positive; most of us would have expected it to be negative. The reporter for *Life* on D-day abandoned journalism; he recognized that experience had gotten away from him and he determined to take time out to think, to study, to catch up with it if he could.

All the ingredients are contained in the elixir of life, but it is we who determine their relative strength, with or without conviction as to who or what is the ultimate mixer.

Pressures that build up on every side often determine action—and in time personality, or lack of it—even though they tend to be tangential, if not unrelated, to essential issues. Thus a kind of superhuman effort to be in everyone's good graces is the contemporary version of ambition in social life. The "political" motive in this broad sense takes the place of Bentham's pain-pleasure principle, extending to every aspect of existence with a quantitative thoroughness that makes his felicific calculus entirely contemporary.

Favoring the "right" people, those with the political-social "in," is the definitive law of those who must succeed, our would-be leaders of today. It excludes spontaneity or generosity, and is pervasive to the point of imminent danger and of ultimate sterility. The political aspirant eschews all disinterested action; he accumulates political capital from what appear to be entirely personal friendships, individual acts of humanity, welfare institutions which he serves. And the pattern is taken over as public relations by the erstwhile private citizen, now alas obsolete, if not extinct.

This insatiable thirst for approval and status kills individuality, destroys independence, and is perhaps basic in the way the most senseless fashions sweep the country. So the glass rage in architecture while we talk about shelters and bombs. So the project rage in foundations while higher education faces the most crucial emergency in the democratic period of its history. And project money goes begging because there just aren't enough projects—not even in the natural sciences.

We have overcalculated, as we overdo so many things; want to be so sure of never giving, or even being suspected of giving, without getting, that we lose all chance of that uncalculated, essentially incalculable return which in the perspective of life tends to be the most significant.

We children of "civilization" have a way of

getting ourselves caught in our own web. Only a major shock seems able to shake us free, to give us back to that nature "whence we sprung," lavish and wasteful to be sure (as we are too, senselessly wasteful) but wasteful in the process of creation.

It is in the nature of that process to be not entirely foreseeable. Carried on at all, it must be carried on "wastefully," prodigally. Only the moneychangers can be sure of their *quid pro quo*. Altogether sure.

"In the air this fall," I wrote in September 1952, "there is more than a new season, more than our private hopes—there is new political hope. One candidate at least for the country's leadership has succeeded in discarding the popular election stratagem of being all things to all men. [Premature, alas; to his own cost and perhaps to ours.] If each of us can divest himself of some small part of old and useless baggage, it may be the way will be cleared toward a new start for the nation itself."

That was a reference to Governor Adlai Stevenson and his large store of wit and of folklore. He had told of the Australian with a new boomerang, who couldn't succeed in throwing the old one away —it always came back. Apparently the thrower never thought of letting it lie while he himself pressed forward.

How many of us, and how often, have found ourselves in the predicament of the Australian? It is the recurring theme of anxious nightmares in which we struggle to the point of exhaustion to carry with us all our impedimenta. It is at the basis of blood feuds in which no one dares to wipe the slate clean, to begin again. So we inherit original sin. And the case history of the Bourbons, of whom it was said they never learned and they never forgot, might well be rewritten for most of us.

Indeed nature itself labors through equinoctial convulsions before it starts the new season and lets the old one die—symbol of the reciprocity of birth and death, of the beginning preceded by an end; each as difficult for us as the other, each indispensable to the creative process, and to the course of individuality, to personality. We live in an age and in a society in which the counter-influences are all but irresistible. For we are at a high point of Anglo-Saxon mechanization, economically and socially, which tends at once to obscure and to exacerbate the travail and the turmoil incident to this period of major transitions. The imperturbability of "good manners" has the more easily become apathy; we have dwelt on negative democracy, on that insignificant "one among millions"; imperceptibly we have induced guilt, accompaniment of growing paralysis and its accelerating cause.

Some such cycle may well have contributed to the tidal wave character of the Industrial Revolution in England and the United States, followed again even now by a forewarned Canada! These countries have supplied in their mores those necessary conditions of mechanization: suppression of mood and emotion, initiative, even the recognition of basic change. These have become expensive materially, dangerous spiritually. We in the United States have huge investments to "protect"; more indispensable gadgets, understood less; waste to increase demand; few ideas, largely epiphenomenal: only the rarest challenge justifies not "being regular." Two functions are decisive—administration and promotion. We talk of leadership when we perform them successfully.

The brilliance of the early mechanical age promised to light the world's darkest corners. Today's glare threatens to blind us, blind us to all but the crassly material. We have transformed the productivity which meant liberation and power into the sterility of the Midas touch.

When and why do we transmute into ultimate ends what clearly are only means? When, as so often, the painful effort of creation yields to the relative ease of procreation, initiative to momentum. Wheels turn faster, ruts get deeper, staying in them seems the better part of valor—until the adventure and the passion are wholly beyond us that lift the spirit to conscious power, the confidence of men made in the image of their Creator.

For it is immensely difficult to find new directions, to make real beginnings. Raw material is inchoate, capable of endless varieties both of ob-

12

servation and organization, requiring fantasy, intellect, sustained will, in a fusion of discovery, collaboration, creation: from the formless unimproved, to the formed yet unforeseen, from inspiration to order in mutual propulsion.

Yet do we with equal reluctance abandon what has run its course, and wrestle with the still potential—pitfalls of inertia to the timid, to the bold opportunities for reasoned change that beckon ceaselessly, our inescapable responsibility for assisting both death and birth.

In the second half of this century of streamlining to automation, the Sphinx's riddle carries its penalty built in: will we, while there is time, achieve the wit, the wisdom, and the stamina to replace momentum with creation, fatalism with insight as the motive power of essential change? Essential to prolong a culture and reorient a world.

To achieve the needed independence of mind and of spirit against the most potent impersonal forces and resistances society has generated since myth yielded to logic is to define personality as the ultimate reliance of democracy, tissue of the sincerity and the resolution that alone can salvage industrial civilization.

CHAPTER

2

AMERICAN DEMOCRACY

From Responsibility and the Sense of Opportunity

to Fear and the Sense of Futility

Democracy was born of men's self-respect as they became conscious of responsibility and dignity, the opportunity of being men. In this country democracy is now seriously endangered by a process of accelerated citizen downgrading; it has developed men's fear of being men.

"Alas, the great times we are living in! We of all people," runs a contemporary epigram with mildly cynical Yiddish insight and pathos, suggesting, as it does, that every opportunity is potentially disaster and every disaster potentially opportunity.

Generally, we are not considered a humorless people, yet we do seem to lack any sense of natural limits. So the biggest and the best have become the Siamese twins of American advertising, and again we reach the strange conclusion that quantity is interchangeable with quality.

The portentous character of the foregoing observations is intensified by existing and evolving conjunctures of less and greater seriousness.

In material things we arrive at a contradiction unnoticed by those contemporary carriers of our culture—the small boys and the salesmen—which is also the basis of much of business and of government philosophy. It may be symbolized in the automobile industry, which assures the car owner not merely that his most economical course is a new car every year but that national prosperity depends on it. The thoughtful explain that the annual car theory—whatever its ultimate validity—is for all practical purposes a necessary corollary of mass production on the American scale. Only the philosopher points out that in peace as in war we are a destroying civilization.

High-powered commercialism and almost mythical wealth make for a leveling conformism under democracy as it is misunderstood in the United States today. We bow like grain stalks in the wind to successive waves of fashion—whether demonstrated-for-speed, streamlined models or indistinguishable front and rear ends; we bow to the tyrannizing conventions of the young—from hot rods to child marriages; we bow to our own conventions of amateur athletics—proven to be not only

15

professional but corrupt; we bow to our latter-day McCarthys and Chamberses, our Budenzes and Bentleys—deeply and publicly self-discredited but riding high on the tide of popular fear subsumed under the title of anti-Communism.

"Communism," on the other hand, as gradually we have grown to use it, has become dreary, monotonous name calling and "the American way of life" stands as its eulogistic opposite. Both terms remain at a shopworn verbal level while we try to lift ourselves by proverbial bootstraps to an emotional pitch that will give them content. In this shabby effort we succeed as might be expected—shabbily; in both cases the real content the words may once have had, has been swept away in tides of self-seeking and bandwagon psychology.

"The American way of life," as conceived by most of us today, means primarily a degree of material well-being which, in the fullness of time, war and the preparation for war can only impair. Those who fight against Communism, both internally and externally, often make common cause with those who fight for loot, under whatever guise, or just for the hell of it. Whence take that inner security of motive, the clear goals and the deep convictions which are basic to fighting strength in war as in peace, in national as in individual life?

Whence indeed! but from the real values of life itself. From exploration, adventure, creation, of which the premise is freedom, including—most importantly—the freedom from clichés.

These real values tend to disappear from "the American way of life" as if proscribed by an accelerating austerity program of spiritual starvation—the road to national deterioration, irresistible as physical starvation and at least as painful, which he who runs may read as well in psychiatry as in history.

Culture of the mind and the spirit is expendable as little or as much as life itself.

In the usual panic to get out from under, a chronic despondency takes over because of what is called "lack of leadership." As we deteriorate progressively—one is tempted to say "deliberately" except that "deliberately" implies thinking, which is shunned at any level—we look to this outside force, this leadership, to resupply without effort on our part all that we have wantonly sacrificed, abandoned without a struggle; the one contribution we are prepared to make is "leadership training."

These words have become part of the stock in trade of "public relations" experts, of professional copywriters, who with soaring eloquence advertise that "Leaders train leaders" in a particular school. No one has apparently remembered that leadership takes more than training and that it may make a substantial difference whom the leaders have to lead.

17

The explanation lies at least in part in a somewhat misunderstood democracy. Leaders are neither born nor made, they have to be both. But the notion with which we have been brought up, that our boys—and soon our girls—can all be President, has been construed to mean, in practice, that they are more or less equally fitted to be. With all of us potential leaders, it then injures self-esteem, and somehow abrogates opportunities that we regard as ours of right, to acknowledge superior men and women. We are just plain afraid of them and, when we can, try to prevent their emerging on the political scene. The result is that most of them no longer try and that the grade of our public servants, whom year after year we elect, is by and large hardly average.

Consider the politics of the most recent New York mayoralty election. The New York *Post*, not uniformly on the side of the angels, summed it up: the Mayor was running against himself. After four years in the office which he was now about to reform, he had become the standard-bearer of the new dispensation, the reform movement of the Democratic Party. He got the endorsements—hallmark of purity—of those two public servants *sans peur et sans reproche*, Mrs. Roosevelt and Governor Lehman. With that clear mandate of, by, and for the people, further fortified by a substantial election majority, he moved promptly to raise his own salary by 40 per cent.

What has become of the builders and frontiersmen we once were? What has happened to the Tom Sawyers, who needed to be shown? To the Ben Franklins, with their tolerance and their spirit of inquiry? To the Tom Jeffersons, and "the strongest government on earth"? Can we no longer acknowledge that there are those who clear the trails to a summit? Must we ignore them, or haul them down in order to feel our God-given equality? Or pretend there is no summit?

The uneven progress and regress of science and society athwart the centuries have produced rugged terrain, calling for giants of intelligence and spirit. Because today we fail to seek them—we even suppress them—so do we fail to find them. We need to accept with fresh courage and with better grace the burdens and the privileges of a citizenry summoned, like Cincinnatus from his plow, to meet the national emergency and the call to world leadership at a historical parting of the ways.

Reverting to Governor Stevenson, we thought we had found each other—or some of us did—the leader and the led, and the core of the American tradition. "Here on the prairies of Illinois and the Middle West we can see a long way in all directions. . . . Here there are no barriers, no defenses to ideas and aspirations. We want none," he said in his welcoming address to the Democratic National Convention in Chicago, 1952. I wrote in December:

. . .

His speeches were a new experience—among others for John Steinbeck. Having read that meetings were quiet because audiences were unmoved, he watched them "leaning forward . . . listening all right, listening as an audience does to fine theatre, fine music, or fine talking."

Listening to their own deepest convictions become articulate, clarified, deepened, as spirits rose, released from an imprisoned century. Then the diffident became sure, the sensitive bold, the thrifty generous, and the generous more generous.

On the night of the nomination we seemed to recognize a leader, and on the night of the election to recognize a friend. The old and young, the poor and rich, the simple and sophisticated, thousands upon thousands of us, more probably millions, experienced the outcome as personal misfortune, not less than national: Stevenson was likely to disappear from the line of vision.

Each in his kind sought to prevent it. With that sense of the earth and those on it occasionally characteristic of the President, Mr. Truman acknowledged him party leader. The British thought of him as ambassador. *The New Yorker*, "lifted, strengthened, reassured," rereading his speeches, offered them as a handbook to the new President. Volunteers proposed to continue in politics; seventy thousand wrote—how many more would have liked to write?

"I ask of you all you have; I will give to you all I have."

Humanity is the deep current of politics. After the years of insistent clamor, suddenly leadership was here—or so we thought—intimate and individual, self-evident and engulfing like the incoming tide lifting the stranded, once again to sail fair and free.

Could the foregoing paragraphs have been written today, more than ten years later? Could one have recaptured the vision of the man of the first campaign after the second? I hardly think so. That transition was hard to make, hard genuinely to follow even while it was in progress.

What had happened? The politicos had convinced Mr. Stevenson that he lacked political sense; he was too idealistic and too highbrow, above the heads and the hearts of the electorate. Then "what a fall was there, my countrymen!" In Mr. Stevenson's search for the largest public, and the lowest common denominator—likely to be futile except in mathematics—he sacrificed his integrity and lost the electorate. He lost those who knew this kind of game, at which he was after all an amateur, therefore playing it harder, as the amateur always does. He lost, too, with a profound sense of reciprocal loss, those who had been "lifted, strengthened, reassured." Their hero had succumbed, succumbed utterly to the notions, first, that national leadership could be acquired by training, by hackneyed political techniques; second, and more important, that personal grandeur was dead, statesmanship outmoded, in that American tradition of his first campaign.

Charles Dickens in *Pickwick Papers* describes the prototype of the American candidate for office, who considers it contrary to all political strategy to deviate from the notion that "a more independent, a more enlightened, a more public-spirited, a more noble-minded, a more disinterested set of men than those who promised to vote for the candidate ever existed on earth." This would be disloyal to the mediocrity we idealize in defense of ourselves.

But in Dickens' day we were nearer to the birth of American democracy. Perhaps it was appropriate over and over again to bring home the fact that government recognized the people who fought for and created it. They were often well led in those days but they were also individually experienced in their politics—or some of them were—interested in their local and their national community. Nearly two hundred years of this glorification of the common man has led variously to inertia, to skepticism, or to overweening self-confidence. Either we want to be leaders, or we want not to be bothered. This gives one kind of leader his opportunity, the leader who likewise does not want to be bothered by those he leads because he knows well enough what is good for them. Especially when the loosening social ties of convulsive change weaken the body politic as it gropes for a new organization of forces.

Inversely to other satisfactions, the pull of power grows with the competitive struggle. Until like the monkey triplets, those in its grip—viz., all but the most exceptional of leaders—speak nothing, see nothing, hear nothing, nothing but the magnetic strains of power, played with the eternal magic of the Pied Piper to his regular following by any other name.

"These are the times that try men's souls," times for the demagogue and the dictator of whom the tyrant of old was no more than the germ. We have seen him take over many times in the course of history, as we have seen him take over in many places during our own lifetime. And still such a takeover remains beyond our visualizing here— not because it is an impossibility but because we are afraid to confront it as a possibility.

Real leaders of a democracy rouse people to action by treating them as full-grown men and women who can be called upon to meet their obligations, colleagues who expect and know how to collaborate. But just as we became aware of this educational principle in relation to our children, we abandoned it in the treatment of our contemporaries. Pericles to the contrary notwithstanding, compensation for frustrations became in mid-century America the secret both of happiness and freedom.

The time has come for the body of our citizens once again to be aware of themselves as co-builders, architects of their own future. The sense of shared responsibility is the matrix of democratic leadership. There is no other.

CHAPTER

CORPORATE ORGANIZATION
AND BUREAUCRACY

"The Trustees Are Responsible":

Collective Responsibility, So-called,

or Irresponsibility

Corporate organization is the legal device widely used to conduct large enterprises—sometimes not so large—especially under capitalist democracy. A group of persons usually known as a board of trustees or directors, constitute themselves a corporation, i.e., a single legal person, chartered to carry out the specific objectives of a given business, philanthropic or educational concern. The board is collectively responsible for its affairs. Corporate administration for the most part has developed in more or less fixed functional hierarchies, collectively referred to as bureaucracy. The corporate form pervades capitalist democracy.

Recent experience furnishes more or less random examples of corporate organization and performance which establish the foundations for the generalizations that follow; they occurred in hospital care, education, business, athletics. The president of the hospital board was intelligent, sensitive to misery, therefore generous to the hospital, unusually capable in business affairs. Yet, during his tenure, unquestionably disinterested professional advice as to material savings in building costs was deliberately ignored—they were "wealthy enough so it didn't matter." Evidence from a friendly source as to the utterly subordinate role—not to say neglect—of the patient in relation to hospital routine, he received or, better, rejected, with such obvious displeasure as to make it immediately advisable to "Save your breath to cool your porridge." During the years since that occurrence, the hospital has gone incredibly downhill in public esteem, and precisely because the patient became a number.

In another of our top hospitals, a departing patient, from one of New York's most prominent and wealthy families, sent for its director to tell him she would in future "consider it her duty to keep out of that hospital anyone whom she could possibly influence." A third had such confidence in its own routine that over the protest of a physician-patient an injection was duplicated with distinctly unpleasant consequences because "No one else *could* have given the injection" except the nurse in question. It goes without saying that a less informed patient might have suffered more serious results because countermeasures might have been delayed.

Anyone with recent hospital experience knows that such incidents are by no means exceptional. The likely answer is shortage of nurses, overwork, etc. Yet with these factors are coupled ironclad rules governing relatives' attendance on patients for even the simplest services. It is apparently preferable to let the patient wait hours, then to wake him in order to give him a sleeping pill, rather than to allow the slightest leeway to persons with primary concern in his recovery.

It may be presumed that a board member's interest in hospitals stems from some kind of hospital experience. Or that if it doesn't he would regard it as his obligation to familiarize himself with ordinary hospital procedures, try to keep in mind that hospitals are supported with public funds, that in the public mind patients are more important than procedures, that membership on the board falls short of omniscience to the extent that the board member fails to keep currently in touch with what is going on at the institution for which in law and in fact he is responsible.

Another board's utterly and continuingly irresponsible role in an educational situation justifies.

development at greater length for the light it sheds on innumerable comparable episodes in the field of higher education—one might almost say that each institution can supply its own episode, often several. The story is in a primary way illustrative of the deteriorating mechanism we have for handling volunteer philanthropic services on which this country has prided itself.

The case concerned the choice of a new head of a distinguished school. The board asked for recommendations from all sources, to be professionally investigated by a man engaged for the purpose, with the final choice to be made by the board from among those who on the record appeared most promising. To assist in the search each of two deans was asked to name an advisory committee.

The board accepted the statement of the retiring president, probably supported by two other officers, that his vice-president was incapable, by reason of being excessively quarrelsome, of taking over the executive function even temporarily. This statement was taken as final, even though less than one year earlier the president had caused the vice-president to cancel a long-prepared and long-postponed vacation so that he might make the journey which would assure his own next job. The vice-president replaced him without incident during his two months' absence.

Accordingly the vice-president proposed that this quarrelsomeness be investigated through two officers, high in board and administration esteem, who had of their own initiative recently withdrawn from the institution and were therefore without personal stake in it. One of these was never approached, the other only after a single board member had more or less insisted on it. But the testimony was ignored as being too favorable to the vice-president and therefore clearly prejudiced.

The next step was the board's election of an acting president without advance notice to the board membership that this election was part of the business of its meeting. The vice-president expressed the hope to the acting president that he would in his new capacity personally acquaint himself with what was going on at the institution. After two or three committee meetings, he was never seen there at all.

Meanwhile the vice-president, who was also one of the two aforementioned deans, submitted to the board the names of an exceptionally distinguished advisory committee, which the board accepted; all of these men had taught at the school for many years. Neither the report of this committee, nor the names it proposed as presidential candidates, were ever solicited.

As rumors persisted about the impending presidential appointment, the vice-president at once sent to each board member by registered mail and special delivery, with accompanying letter, copies of the advisory committee report, each hand-signed by the members of the committee and likewise containing their recommended names—two men of high administrative and academic repute. Letter, names, report, were ignored completely: no reference was ever made to them nor explanation offered either to the vice-president or the committee.

The man named to the presidency was one of the deans. He had been with the institution for a year and a half. His appointment had seemed likely after the man paid to do the "screening" had stated that the best candidate was "right there in the institution all the time." In response to the vice-president's question as to the extent of the board's investigation of the candidate's record, the answer was (1) The members of the committee had been questioned whom the candidate had appointed as advisory in his earlier capacity as dean. (2) The board had no need to investigate since they had so carefully looked into his outside record a year and a half earlier, before he came to the school. And, finally, the man paid to do the screening had found no other name worthy of the board's consideration, among all those submitted. In short, the very best one could say of the appointment was that it was made by the paid screener. If this appears unlikely, there are other hypotheses.

Although the acting president was the chief protagonist, the working group was a triumvirate consisting of a front, of a brain—ruthless, astute— and of a public-relations type. The plan in essence was provided by the absentee ex-president, lobbying by mail. The utter bankruptcy of the appointment resulted in the new president's "resignation" two years later. The erstwhile acting president, now chairman of the board, continues with relentless effort and identical standards of conduct to try to foist his will on the institution. Unusual in the situation is that he has roused the moral conscience of one or two of his colleagues. The outcome is still unclear at this writing.

A prominent museum made the headlines. For years it had been working on plans for a new building with that nearly incredible travail which only genius can provide, especially architectural genius, genius on a scale that knows no law, least of all building law. The museum director agonized through those three or four years. An unusually urbane man in the normal course, he had reached the point where it was impossible to spend an evening with him without "giving him the floor" for a couple of hours. As he phrased it, it was the only way he could unwind.

When the architect's attention was called to things so irrelevant as requirements of the building law or of the museum's collections, his answer was always the same: they were not his concern. That the museum finally opened with stunning success was owing solely to the director's merit, to his tenacity and his determination, his control and his intelligence, his expertness and his good

31

taste, and above all, his sheer devotion.

With the opening of its new quarters, the museum was for weeks in what one can only describe as a state of siege. For the first time in its history admission was charged. Professional and lay comment was for the most part equally enthusiastic.

Well before a year had elapsed, the museum made its next headline with the dismissal of the director. The date of his leaving was set prior to the opening of the important international award exhibit which was entirely his work.

The excesses of amateur sports, largely the responsibility of the colleges, must be laid at the door of boards of trustees and alumni, always partially overlapping. To award scholarships for athletic prowess is recognized common practice. With this largest reward the colleges can give for excellence on any of a number of teams, went the basketball bribery scandals which revealed that, for a given sum, players were persuaded by gamblers to reduce the winning margin or throw the game to the rival contestants. This is the perversion that has come of the original idea of cultivating sportsmanship in the best sense—it should include skill, honesty, and the generosity of knowing equally how to win or to lose; something like the modern equivalent of chivalry.

In its excesses—one hardly knows whether to laugh or to cry—overemphasis of athletics has emerged in Africa recently, where it has become identified with national instead of merely college prestige, and has assumed proportions one could hardly credit except for Lloyd Garrison's signed report from Brazzaville on the first page of the Sunday *Times* of September 23, 1962: "Gabon expelled 3,000 residents today because of a misunderstanding about a soccer match. . . . The refugees arrived by ship at Pointe Noire. . . .

"In Brazzaville today frightened Gabonese immigrants locked their doors and sought refuge with the police in fear of retaliation. . . .

"All over Africa winning has become a matter of national honor. No elected official would dare dispute a government's decision to spend thousands of dollars to train a national team and pay large salaries for foreign coaches. . . .

"In Ghana and Guinea . . . [coaches] are usually dismissed and sent home if their teams lose twice in a row. . . .

" 'There are two things every diplomat, no matter what his nationality, dreads more than anything else short of war,' a British diplomat commented. 'One is for your country to dispatch a good will naval visit and give 3,000 of your sailors shore leave. The other is to try to build international friendship through football.' "

While my own intimate milieu is not business, a recent, essentially "everyday" experience with it makes vivid from yet another angle in what diverse ways wealth, waste, materialism, and frustration eat away time—and so life—destroy ideals, erode character, blur judgment as to what is essential and what is secondary, wrong and right, good and bad.

A commonplace story—rental of an apartment, medium price. It contained, among other things, a wall of built-in bookcases, and half-sized window guards on street-level windows, necessary for protection in an increasingly lawless city, especially with a small child living there; the burly superintendent, occupying a street-level apartment, had them on his windows.

A request to the agent, "Can we have full window guards?"

"We'll discuss that after you move in."

Repainting was about to start, with it a request as to color of bookshelves.

Answer: "They're probably torn out."

"How is that possible, you say the tenants just moved out—will you please find out and let me know at once."

After a couple of hours another telephone call to the renting agent, "I haven't had time to find out, I'll send someone down right away." A little later, "They've destroyed some of the shelves but we can leave the frame in."

There followed a $10 tip to the superintendent, who promised completion of work in the apartment by a given date. Intervening telephone check-ups confirmed that all was going as promised,

"We just have to clean up."

Following the "cleanup" day, no cleaning, no stove, no door that would close, and an extremely disagreeable, irritated superintendent.

Then the discovery that the window guards had been removed completely. The superintendent's explanation, "No one told us to leave them up; it will take ten days to get them."

Repeatedly, as I waited in the office to get the attention of the authorities, I heard the basic philosophy of the hard-pressed personnel: "The more you remove from an apartment, the fewer the occasions for complaints."

This concentrated period of moving in and moving out is also the employees' harvest period. Each and every service, however slight, wants to be assured a tip; hence in this particular building the working personnel was constantly being exchanged in the various apartments, and nerves were taxed almost beyond endurance. Yet even under the most favorable circumstances the ordinary complement of porters and handymen cannot handle the workload of September-October.

Returning to my specific apartment, the youth bed ordered from a well-known department store failed to arrive. That store takes as long to answer the telephone as Western Union, with the difference that when they do answer, they often say they will have to call back. I told Mrs. X the bed had not arrived as promised:

35

"Yes, I know, they are four hundred deliveries behind at that factory on account of illness, but they are hoping for the complete staff by Monday. I could connect you with the complaint department but they will only give you the run-around; they never do anything about a delivery until it is at least ten days late."

I blessed her, not unaware like the Ancient Mariner, but exuberantly. Never before had I, in a similar situation, encountered anyone who thought it mattered whether or not I spent most of my waking life holding a telephone receiver, it might be (1) patiently waiting, (2) impatiently or patiently complaining, (3) listening to professionally courteous, meaningless reassurance, (4) or listening to the vocally endowed bureaucratic wall; or, seriatim, all four.

In the age of efficiency and gadgets a technology has been worked out for weakening the fiber of complainers, to such a point that there are those among us who feel that the choice is between "Do it yourself" and abandoning the gadget—they refuse to face the repair services.

The single success I can record with a repair service, came through ignoring successive bills for repeated repairs to a washing machine. On what proved to be a mechanic's final visit, this particular one said he had instructions to collect the bills. I assured him I would pay no more than one bill.

Would I speak to the man in charge in the office?

"Nothing," I said, "would please me more." Here was my chance to skip over the smaller bureaucrats to the small bureaucrat! My pent-up emotions attained such eloquence that the only reply I got from the other end ran: "Will you please pay our man for the single service."

As I left the laundry "our man" remarked to a bystander, "That's a very intelligent lady." But it was only potential transformed into kinetic energy.

Before proceeding to the second part of this chapter, it should be explicitly stated that there are of course exceptional corporations just as there are exceptional people.

Linguistically, philanthropy derives from love of humanity. So should it factually, mitigating as far as possible, at times circumventing, the inexorable one-dimensionality of time in whatever partial escape from the consequences of one's own acts or of outside events.

Humanism so conceived is what makes life livable in any of its aspects; it may even be what makes it sane, effective. Like most of our observations, this becomes increasingly clear as humanism approaches the vanishing point in more and more areas of living, and one is left gradually with the feeling that only a new era of Biblical prophecy can save us.

Whatever in these days pertains to individuals as individuals gravitates toward pejorative functional and ethical implications as, e.g., in the contrasting connotations, in many areas, of humanism and planning. The latter suggests unbiased evaluation of needs to be met on their merits, the former unpredictable, because ungeneralized and therefore putatively prejudiced, motives for action. The complexity of the human situation is left out of account, which in specific instances may make it humanly incompatible with a given principle. In terms of the more intimately personal motive, planning tends to avoid frustration in the godlike role of the planner; humanism is said to "manipulate" humanity in the interest of a particular, preconceived goal, pure egotism is the third way. Primary impetus in each may be generated more impersonally, more humanly, or with a shorter focus on self.

The planner is organized, systematic, constantly enlarging his view to find the ideal relationships of more and more things, facilities, activities, people, groups. As the environment he creates grows increasingly effective, the life he makes possible becomes externally more agreeable, more varied, and yet in some sense more uniform. But basically he deals with the inanimate; even when he provides for people most sensitively, he works not with them but for them: they answer back only as he lets them. Notwithstanding that he often feels an irreducible stubbornness even in things as such, it is a work milieu more susceptible of order, simpler to that extent. And if the tolerance for frustration somehow correlates with optimism and faith, then it may be the planner also carries a large component of pessimism.

Of comparable orientation is the administrator, devoted to the point of impersonality to the institution for which he feels responsible, under the procedures he recognizes as good. Continuing deviation from the course, from proved or preferred methods, is betrayal, violation of principle and primary loyalty. This is neither a tenable situation nor one that too often may be permitted to arise, for to him it is destruction itself. This man or woman of unyielding principle—"relativist" or "absolutist"—becomes ruthless, little or much, late or soon. The relativist arrives at his stand generally by logic and philosophy, as rigidly, it may be, a man of principle in practice as he is without it in theory. The believer in absolute good, reaching his position by a kind of ethical-psychological instinct, may none the less conceive of it in the most varied forms, basically confident that he will always and everywhere recognize a really good man.

The humanist's field of action is people, of whom each is as little subject to direct, consistent, overall planning as freedom itself, the human mainspring. To deal with people is to take account of them as personalities, allowing for their individuality, indeed ministering to it insofar as it does not excessively interfere with pursuing common goals; influencing and being influenced. Issues are presented as far as possible in individual terms of reference, only then and from there leading on and up to what is universally more meaningful. This is a process requiring understanding and patience, sensitivity, resourcefulness, constant adaptation, and the courage to confront an endless lack of finality. To call the process manipulation (as it often is called) is to select negatively among the factors that make it up; depending on the sensitivity and the honesty with which it is used, it may indeed be more appropriately thought of as the antithesis of manipulation, as the effort to make a given situation clear to a given intelligence and temperament.

Obviously it is much easier to operate on principle, to ignore the unique character of a set of circumstances, to shut out or at least keep at arm's length its individual human elements for the sake of the "greatest good of the greatest number" for whom corporate boards of trustees legislate and plan with a kind of exalted omniscience in each case that fortifies feelings of superiority and power. Status is enhanced by membership on such a board of one's peers; members negotiate as equals except that "some are more equal than others," according to one astute observer. They "trade" in the spirit of their world, which is business, only without controls because it is on the philanthropic exchange.

In contact with just a limited number of comparable élites, the board of each agency is like an independent principality or an oligarchy, depending on the distribution of power. The prestige of this aristocracy is largely what motivates the philanthropist and explains his psychological profile. Important to him, for the most part, is less whom he is working for than whom he is working with. The credentials are socio-economic almost exclusively, with position counting, rather than personality, except in the rarest instances. And again we have lost the individual—even in a small and otherwise "manipulative" area.

On the whole the individual in his individuality is a nuisance to the bureaucracy. He tends to disagree, to arouse troublesome sympathies, to get in the way of decisions on principle and accepted ways of spending money, to point up shortcomings —literally to make more trouble than a regiment.

The bureaucrat is prone to forget that it is not only the affairs of true love that never did run smooth but the affairs of the living altogether. As we don't like machines that do the unexpected, neither do we like people who do. What happens to our efficiency when we cannot treat them en masse—make one virtuous decision for all!

A closer look at the bureaucracy is indicated. The top bureaucrat clearly takes it out on the lower levels in all good faith. Presumably he is a good executive or he would not enjoy that position. Good executives are scarce, as we all know. But while some retain their posts for substantially all of their working life, others seek wider areas of usefulness, find it personally more profitable to change, or from the outset consider a government post the means to an end, a way to prestige and influential contacts. Numbers of these top officials proceed as if the world had been created yesterday or, better, were to be created tomorrow. The fewest call upon their subordinates to orient them in the agency's accumulated experience. They have been appointed on their own merits and they will radically avoid bogging down in whosever antiquated prejudices.

The small bureaucrat preys on the public, more damned today by far than when Commodore Vanderbilt publicly announced his policy. To be sure the outward and visible signs have changed in favor of a courtesy (described above) so frictionless as to defy contact, and for this consumer at least, much harder to take than out-and-out war. It is a government legacy to the people, invented by the dictators, happily absorbed by the democracies, thence filtered down to every form of bureaucracy where it may seem profitable. "Do nothing but do it courteously and keep your own counsel." Thus your victim receives the gift of endless hope, i.e., provided he has not been exposed too often.

Strange that in our preoccupation with the

atomic age we have forgotten the atom, forgotten that this infinitesimal particle of matter is the source of ultimate power. If we remembered, we might not despair of the human individual, neglect or ignore him, regard him as the powerless victim of a negative selection of the goals he has envisioned and the methods he has employed, translate mass production as the source of material strength into notions of mass education as the source of spiritual strength; we might not stress applied research to the point of forgetting that what we are applying are the findings of basic research; and in the final inversion of process and meaning, we might not have borne the idea that the machine may well supplant its creator.

All this in the context of the Copernican counter-revolution, Freud's discovery that not our planet but ourselves, each of us, is the center of our universe. And that the pattern of our relations to others—success, leadership, morality—depends, first and last, on the central relation to oneself. In this new birth of freedom Archimedes for a moment found his lever and found it to be spiritual. But the new fear engulfed the new hope—the fear that a mechanized and mechanistic culture, glorified beyond reason or recognition, threatened the self with extinction.

We are in a situation in which, however defiantly serious the issues, we can scarcely avoid raising the question of fashion and how far we are

43

justified in following it. At least in psychological fashion it may be presumed that there is enough of basic thought involved, now as before, to preclude another swing from extreme to extreme, from nearly exclusive emphasis on the self, hence on the individual, to the statistical mass and the questionnaire as the measure of all things, in an attempt to fit what remains of a human world into a "mechanical brain." As if a brain could be mechanical!

But of all such extreme logical—or illogical—alternatives, probably none is more fraught with incalculable potential for ill than excessive glorification either of the individual or of the mass. Each in its own way is pregnant with ultimate evils: of dictatorship and power; of huge or tiny empires and bureaucracies, political and economic; of suppression of individuality or its abuse; of unfed because unnoticed, and therefore rapidly exhausting wellsprings, of creativity. In another Robert Frost phrase "a population homogenized to the point where the cream will never again rise to the top."

The philanthropist is often the extreme case to document this polarization from which we in the United States suffer. Because of his good works he feels himself righteously beyond the law. With a few of his peers, fully confident and sovereign, he makes, or disregards, the laws of his organization on issues and people and situations that often he neither knows nor investigates, completely satisfied because ignorant that he does not know. Yet

44

he should by definition be the humanist. This he has long since forgotten, if indeed he ever knew, for high-level corporate bureaucracy is the ideal on which he has grown to "maturity." One recalls the case of the young collegian whose father "refused to worry about his son's radicalism—he was destined for banking where such views are bound to disappear."

The board member brings to philanthropy, lock, stock, and barrel, his bureaucratic ideal, complete in all save specific competence and personal risk. To have been successful in business is presumptively to be successful in whatever he may choose to undertake of corporate organization. And so as a trustee in the large range of nonprofit enterprises, he may sink or save his particular project with equal conviction and self-righteousness, aware only after the fact which it has been—and perhaps not even then, nor whose the responsibility. His clique provides the support for his snobbery in attitude and his intrigue in action. This he substitutes for the effort of fair judgment after looking fairly into the facts. To the extent that the clique takes over, the enterprise goes down, in sincerity, effectiveness, distinction, from the level of ideas and ideals of its initiators.

The things we know on earth have their earth-bound trajectory. But how long they travel, how high, and how far is not completely determined by their initial momentum. A spiritual component in human affairs, changing with changing personnel, supplies a necessary line of force approaching the vertical according to its strength; without it there is no prolonged rise above the surface: it is the essence of humanism.

CHAPTER

4

THE RUNAWAY MIRED

Vigilance Cries Out for Reason

to Temper Momentum

An age of transition takes its toll especially in the effort that living demands. Gravitating, as we do today, between visions of ultimate calamity and a new magic bounded only by the reach of human imagination, the spirit struggles with a profound weariness to do no more than hold its own. And "life's fitful fever" once again uncovers the basic significance of "the golden mean": assuming comparable motivation, it is center spectrum that is uniquely congenial—our senses themselves are unequipped for the high and low frequencies. Physically we lose them, ethically the extremes even of virtue become vice.

We have known this explicitly for twenty-three centuries; yet when we need most to be aware of it, in practice we most ignore it, to the point of theorizing about relativism. Action, to be sure, implies an actor for its definition, and the rate of motion varies with a man, an earthworm, or a star: each has its related range which we are unlikely to confuse with another's, but relation need imply nothing of relativism, notwithstanding a common derivation. Language, well-used, is one of the miracle tools of culture; used without precision or, worse, without respect, it is equally miraculous in the havoc and confusion with which it enhances difficulties from whatever source, or creates them.

Slowly and steadily, then with increasing acceleration, the pace of life has increased from paleolithic times, until today we are disposed to think of ourselves as victims of a runaway world rather than prime movers in bringing it about—runaway and mired concurrently in unsynchronized motion and treadmill repose.

The thoughtful metropolitan dweller is constantly moved to re-examine his position: are his three- or four-score and ten being dissipated by an infinitude of secondary activities and complexities that are all but irresistibly controlling? Confronting the stubborn facts of daily living, one encounters—or did encounter—the equally stubborn cliché, "We cannot stop the wheels of progress." *Did encounter*, because latterly the legitimacy of referring to progress is being questioned; no one questions our inability to stop or even slow the wheels, i.e., no one publicly, but L. Harrison Matthews, Fellow of the Royal Society, Director of the Zoological Society of London, at the 121st meeting of the British Association for the Advancement of Science, reported in *The New York Times* of September 4, 1959: "A British scientist warned today that unless the tempo of life slackened in the next few years, the population of the United States and Europe might suffer a catastrophic crash because of mass neuroses."

A discovery as reassuring as devastating, depending on whether the response is human, i.e., intelligent, or reflex—sheer momentum.

The evidence is overwhelming: who has a few weekend hours for the deep, inner calm of country silence? Wider expanses of sky? Longer perspectives? Undisturbed time with a friend? With any nonmechanical occupation? Crucial, perhaps—with oneself?

In some such essentially simple terms neuroses, the diseases of tension, are ours to prevent. It is our responsibility and our prerogative, core of personality and freedom. Yet what we confront is its opposite, a patterned mass compulsion—neurosis.

The reasons, although complex in detail, root in the tempo of industry, the ideal of mass consumption, and the special brand of materialism which the economy of abundance—or of waste— has foisted upon us. As an attitude toward life, this materialism is identified with money rather

49

than what money buys, and both contribute to prestige. The forms prestige takes are often more crudely competitive than the potlatch from which they descend; the virtue of 1964 as compared with 1963 model cars presents the anomaly of a materialism that destroys respect for the material. A parenthesis on the subject of cars: they recur frequently in the text as perhaps the most telling symbol of our culture, inescapably in the experience of all of us. One might, but for that, have chosen nylon hose, originally heralded for their wearing qualities—now made with the definitive purpose not to wear. Or television sets, of which, to avoid friction, one begins to be required for each of us, further atomizing our society and making it more and more conformist at the same time.

In a related development we are well on the way toward a democracy without respect for the individual whom in the mass it pretends to idealize. And so respect is destroyed altogether—including self-respect—as we have consented to become objects rather than subjects, whether of vote getters, advertising campaigns, or large-scale mechanical toys from motorcars to TV.

Consider a few random facts:

1. The continuing traffic slaughter.
2. The continuing traffic tension (in cities).
3. The huge numbers of the mentally ill.
4. The inflation nightmare, oblivious of nonproductive, sky-rocketing costs of promotion.

5. Acknowledged lack of incentive and inner cohesion in labor's ranks whenever material gains have been achieved.

6. Lack of discrimination on those unnumbered TV man hours of our citizenry, present and future.

Not death, but mass consumption—aiming for progressively lower, because putatively larger, targets—is the great leveler, while the nation, nay the planet, remains the quasi-paralyzed audience of the mass communications industries. Our modern-day Belshazzar's Feast is the so-called American standard of living. Has the handwriting on the wall to remain always invisible? Forever?

"Eternal vigilance is the price of liberty." More than a century has elapsed since John Philpot Curran found the formulation that should be graven on the heart of every American. Yet neither heart nor brain has grasped it, and Curran did not go far enough: sustained by resolute courage, eternal vigilance is the price of life itself.

Whether in health or in business, in the professions or in sports, in institutions or in individuals, there is small likelihood that we can maintain our position if we do not also advance it. The most accomplished musician, like the most accomplished baseball player, practices for the duration of his professional life. The businessman or the manufacturer who adheres to the tastes or the methods of his father soon finds he has run his course. The lawyer, the scientist, the scholar, even the daily reader of the news, would occasionally like to halt the presses. The orphanages, the jails, the hospitals, the very apartment houses of yesterday, are the anachronisms of today.

Even so fragmentary a glance at the unremitting struggle leaves us gasping; a human pace is essential to a human scale. Yet who has attempted —and why—squarely to meet the deadly menace of continuing acceleration? The industrialist whose plant is threatened by an invention with too quick an obsolescence may temporarily suppress it if he can, as witness the early history of television—or the distributor of a widely marketed product whose promotion investment would be wiped out by a more effective replacement. But the greater danger is not financial, it is spiritual; and the method—if not the motive—points to the future.

In pace we have come in many areas to the point of diminishing or even negative returns; to the point of choice, therefore, between acceleration and deceleration, between stepping down certain activities for more productive results, or because certain others demand the same or increased performance.

Erich Leinsdorf, conductor of the Boston Symphony Orchestra, wrote in an article in the *Atlantic Monthly* some years ago, "Let there be no doubt that the desire for great native artists can be fulfilled only when the talents who live in our midst in great numbers are permitted to develop as artists. That does not mean they need ivory towers. It merely means that the largest part of their working lives should be spent in freedom from business, in freedom from administration, in freedom from worries of promotion, advertising, meetings. . . ."

The man from Mars taking a look at the collective activities we know as promotion would find them expendable. Not we. The more we promote, the more others promote; and the more, in turn, do we have to promote or think we do. We meet the paper barrage with more paper, advertise in the press the television advertising and vice versa, counter the essential complications with avoidable ones. Vigilance cries out for reason to temper momentum; failing it, to face inevitable disaster.

In terms of physics, momentum and inertia are related phenomena: each is the continuance of a pre-existing state, whether of motion or rest. These two phenomena have been less identified in culture, perhaps because it is acceleration or deceleration that actually occurs.

But spiritually acceleration is a form of momentum—instead of doing just the same, it is doing more of the same, with some intervention of initiative, to be sure, but a minimum. What starts out as a good or even a great idea is ridden to death for failure basically to re-examine it. Moreover, we tend to think of progress as quantitative, to praise our greater and growing accomplishment, to defend it vehemently if it is attacked.

We are living out the acceleration of the Industrial Revolution, and perhaps its decline, unless we take the responsibility for influencing its rate and its direction. Renaissance Europe became in the ensuing centuries a museum on a continental scale, motivated largely by individual self-aggrandizement, and exploded when larger numbers of selves demanded their due. Earlier empires succumbed to their own cumulative conquests.

Perhaps the evidence is at least suggestive, grounds for raising the question whether progress is not to be defined rather by deliberate breaks in momentum than by the competitive instinct blindly and continuously to speed up what in moderation has been a blessing.

The great man is generally distinguished by instinctive simplicity, the need and the ability to isolate essentials from the complications in which they are embedded. This is what moves him and the world forward, what establishes the conditions for creation. We, too, the rank and file of us, have such an obligation to the extent of the ability we command. The stake is *true* progress, the good life for which we have the essentials if we will take time and responsibility for finding out what they are; if we do not assume that because one motorcar can move us faster and farther than a horse and wagon, we shall go correspondingly faster and farther with millions of motorcars long after they have come to a dead stop in our city streets, or have slain tens of thousands for the adventure of speed on the open road.

Knowledge and techniques that are new, and taken seriously, reorient thinking, the thinking of the developing mind coming abreast of its inheritance, the thinking of the human race enlarging the periphery of the known. But, taken superficially, what the new appears to produce most simply and naturally is new clichés by which men tend to live—or step by step to die.

Source par excellence of new knowledge and invention, the play instinct at its purest, and at all ages, is ceaselessly exploring, ceaselessly creating. But to regularize its use, to write the rules of the new game, to distinguish the significant from the negligible, requires a degree of penetration, perseverance, sincerity which is of a different order from following rules already established. We are doing neither. Propelled in action by simple momentum, in thought by the potent seduction of the comprehensive hypothesis, taking more and more into account with decreasing rigor (or less and less with decreasing integration), we lump together all our problems of reorientation, ignore or slight such precise knowledge as we do have, then talk sophisticatedly about relativism.

Philosophy and psychology, ethics and semantics—misunderstood science—have at the same time been carrying on the search for standards, lost in a misdirected effort to find them. Historically the rigidities of Puritanism gave way to new conceptions of mental and physical health, fathered by James, Dewey and Freud; to the surface sophistication of progressively educated youth; to ideas of "relativity," made current by Einstein, but not comprehensible, while the warnings of semantics about the pitfalls of language precipitated the very errors they were designed to avoid.

Had thinking, indeed, its own seismograph, it would record in twentieth-century America one of those major tremors in which mountains sink into the sea. New and major contours emerge— of illness, character, free will. We contribute to our own illness in this changed world; illness was formerly God's exclusive responsibility. Society bears much of the blame for vice and crime, formerly our own responsibility. Deep and persistent neuroses are scarcely distinguishable from character; resentment, indignation prove self-defeating, punishment largely anachronistic and futile. Spiritual problems tend to become health problems; ethical problems as such to disappear.

But if the will to health is strategic for health, and if physical shock may be usefully applied to persistent neurotic states of mind, then the significance must be redefined of the distinction between functional and organic disturbance, the roles of patient and physician, the art of medicine, the science, the humanity. Failure of the will to health may range from hypochondria to denial or creation of symptoms, from belligerent rejection of psychiatry to lifelong dependence on the psychiatrist.

These are the new concepts by which mental hygiene has attempted a revolutionized analysis of daily conduct. It has, however, omitted from its efforts toward new understanding the juxtaposition of extremes to which the contemporary world increasingly exposes us: the good fortune that may be excessive for personal equilibrium, and the momentum we seem to generate toward periodic disaster as the heroic but unconscious remedy for our daily sins. Disaster evokes humanity's highest performance, while milder forms of adversity are discouraging if not demoralizing. And success is said to be the yeast of regular accomplishment, while we rarely measure up to large and unexpected good fortune.

Consciously or unconsciously we blame ourselves for milder frustrations, praise ourselves for the smaller successes. But fate's more telling blows reach beyond personal responsibility and we refuse to succumb to them if we are strong. The area of resistance, defined by what produces it, gives direction to counter-measures and clarifies goals. Misfortune, provided it is still on a human scale, elicits a deeper response the greater the danger—

more direct, more essential, adding to stature.

Contrast the effects of comparable good fortune. Accession of social, political, economic power or distinction opens up larger possibilities and wider environments, opportunities of which we cannot at once avail ourselves because they demand a scale of values that has first to be built. A sensed inadequacy makes for uncertainty which we try to conceal. Temporarily at least it decreases confidence. Our vaunted American standard of living in many respects has been no more than superficially absorbed: only the extremes of poverty legitimately permit identification of material well-being with the good life. Otherwise, to make this egregious error is a basic and disastrous confusion of ends and means, is never to have learned what makes the thrill and the heart of the human adventure.

Civilization is rocking on its foundations in widening swings. We tend to fall into the rhythm: the centrifugal energy of new situations and very partially assimilated knowledge is reinforced with language that hides the lack of thought, with the sanction and the momentum of relativism, in synchronizing vibrations that may send us over the edge.

To the extent that we can make our basic attitudes conscious and bring them profoundly abreast of what is known, each has to himself and his time the moral responsibility of determining whether he is object or subject—the area is equally exploited and exploitable by expert, consumer, promoter, negatively or positively—a disappearing island of free will left from a great continent of other times and other views if we choose to regard ourselves as object; or a new land mass on the horizon if we can see ourselves as subject, a land mass destined to grow as we approach it and stop hugging the shore of a false security of habit, to become reanimated by the agelessly changing adventure of freedom.

5

RETREAT FROM REASON

They Do It at Their Peril

The irrational, or nonrational, has a variety of contemporary excuses, and emphases: on emotion, on action—by trial and error, on intuition, on mysticism, on instinct and the subconscious as its firm foundations.

My adult life has about coincided with the advent and spread of psychoanalysis. Notwithstanding its viewpoint has proved basic in the very conception of man, its misunderstanding has been primary in the sanction of the nonrational in this country, and in its popularity. In my own case, it was only a very few years ago that the formal application of learned symbols to "subconscious" life yielded with sudden conviction to inner understanding.

With all the élan of such a discovery I spoke to Elizabeth Sifton, my wisest friend, of the keenest, most incisive intellectuality. "This is self-revelation, understanding, insight—one's own code, and at a depth I never knew!" "Of course it is," as if self-evident.

Yet nowhere have I seen it stated that the subconscious is irrational only in form, sensitive as a photographic plate to its inner and outer environment, sure, revelatory, and rational in its reactions as its owner's capacity for inner concentration, his degree of interpretive skill, his will to truth, and his courage. Our age has thus enlarged the conscious spiritual world in the continuing process of rediscovery, grasping the deeper meaning of the "irrational" as the primeval shorthand of reason—rediscovery because our remote ancestors believed instinctively in the irrational, generally lacking the art to interpret, with the technique still undeveloped.

But we have our primitives today as we had them in the pre-recorded millennia, those who, ignoring time and knowledge, seize as new on the irrational in its most superficial and dangerous aspects: the religious mystic of these times unwittingly makes common cause with the demagogue and both with the disheartened to extol the non-rational as primary wisdom, adding a new and crushing load to that accumulation of ignorance and error under which we already tell ourselves we must succumb. Railing against the contradictions and the dead ends they encounter, or substituting the simple singleness of fanaticism for the penetration, the will, and the perseverance to trace, to isolate and deal with varied causes, they accelerate magnetically and with self-conscious virtue in that very direction of the irrational we are seeking to avoid.

They do it at their peril. From the Roman Empire, back into the mists of prehistory, forward to the "one-thousand-year Reich," retreat from reason has meant disaster. Divinity itself may not ignore achievements of earlier creation. And we approach Divinity as we understand and heed the moving forces in surrounding worlds, forever surfacing from unplumbed depths. . . .

The Sentence, a play by Franstisek Lange, illustrates in this sense the ultimacy of that need for justice upon which has been built the conscience of mankind.

It opens with the unintentionally fatal assault on a despicable old man-about-town in the room of a showgirl. His assailant is her true lover, an honest, simple-minded waiter. The old man's death is made to appear accidental and everyone is happier for it. His widow breathes more freely; his fortune begins to do some real good; the waiter marries the girl. But as the years pass he finds himself unable to live with himself. In desperation he gives himself up to the police. Following an investigation, they refuse to credit his story. Beside himself, hunted more remorselessly than by posse or bloodhound, he errs endlessly among forgotten quarters and people of the city. Under a bridge he meets a shattered old man, once a judge, shattered, as he tells us, by the futility and the mischief of his profession of pronouncing sentence.

The waiter tells his story. The judge sets time and place for the trial, formal and complete with witnesses. It is held under the bridge with the deep solemnity that springs from the ultimate need of the two principals. For the waiter, expiation, justice; for the judge, goal of a lifelong search: a man whom his profession can genuinely serve, one who needs desperately to be sentenced.

That waiter had the clarity to recognize what most of us ignore, that it is hardest to forgive one-self—if not impossible. One is generally a too much interested party to believe in one's own forgiveness. Our notion of justice as an eye for an eye goes back too far, perhaps to creation itself. Too far, at all events, to permit us to escape applying it to ourselves, knowingly or unknowingly, inexorably, for sins large, small and imagined.

"Use every man after his desert, and who should 'scape whipping?" Plainly no one. And the whipping we do escape is only the sentence; we never escape the verdict of that native subconscious court of primordial justice with its docket of un-numbered acts of which overtly we never suffered the full consequences. Not the fateful inheritance from a remote ancestry in the Christian sense of original sin makes up our burden of guilt, but simply the things we have done or not done for which we never paid the price, regardless of whether there was anyone to pay.

Conscious resentment against the rest of humankind is the other side of the coin. "They" much more obviously than "we" are getting by without paying, at our expense or someone's else. So gossip concerns itself with the suckers, those who by definition cannot help being cheated; and indignation with a kind of high-level resentment in which one's own group seems regularly to be victimized by others.

Psychoanalysis pointed out that guilt and censure often spring from a single source, but the source was the somewhat arbitrary, individual conscience rather than the universal conscience of mankind, the responsibility of man to his maker and to his fellow man. Thus has psychoanalysis often intensified the problem it has only begun to explain: never was a generation more ego-conscious and engrossed, more resentful, more easily frustrated, individually or socially. And the rat race has a meaning as exact as in the laboratory, more pointedly significant for being self-constructed.

Slowly some of the ancient wisdom is infiltrating—too slowly, perhaps often not so wisely, sometimes with new insights. "Example is better than precept," "Judge not that ye be not judged," having failed as practical ethics, are being validated as mental health. We regard it as our twentieth-century discovery that the strongest man will not grow from the most censured child. But what nourishes growth in youth and what impedes it nourishes or undermines equally the stamina and the productivity of age. Resentment engenders resentment and drains the springs of creation in an original chain reaction as old as the world.

Will we ignore this potent reservoir of wisdom newly accessible in the subconscious while resentment accelerates, unbroken, to planetary explosive power with or without the compounding force of atomic energy? Are we in America too prosperous to save ourselves, and others too impoverished? America and Americans are generous, almost in proportion to their wealth. We have the knowledge and the means, we still lack the basic insight, the vision, the confidence, and the practicing humanity, to be generous in a generous spirit, individually, in groups, and as a nation:

Touch us again with immortality;
Give back the upward looking and the light.
Rebuild in us the music and the dream.

In this contemporary ascendancy of the non-rational, emotions have once again received not merely their due but their undue meed. At their humanistic zenith in the Romantic period following the Age of Reason, they appear to have reached their nadir under the exploitation of contemporary dictatorships. The new medievalism may well run on for a new "dark age" if we fail in that "eternal vigilance, the price of freedom."

Action, activity for its own sake, tends also toward its own irrationalism, that either-or method of reasoning which argues that the alternative must be good which we have not recently tried just because its opposite proved bad in our experience. Many of us in this country, fortifying psychoanalysis with progressive education, have thrown out mind in favor of the emotions and of action, with enthusiasm and thoroughness. The outcome in American politics has been the style of Senator McCarthy of blessed memory, Father Coughlin, and Huey Long. Their progeny are still with us even if in the less heroic mold of such as Governor Faubus, Senator Eastland, and underworld demagogues from Apalachin to the teenage gang leadership.

Intellect unrooted in emotion misses conviction, to be sure, and the cohesive power for unified action. But human life is not calculated to be purely one thing or purely another: purity is sterile and extremes tend to be self-contradictory. Surrendering to emotions unsupported by intellect, we stand ready to be victimized by our own anxiety or hero worship, thus by the most naïve devices of tear jerking and oratory, "A road into gathering darkness whence it is said that none return"—at least not by their own efforts during their own lifespan.

Failure for the most part to make rational use of that "subconscious," inside track to our real, most sensitive, most rational selves accounts largely for our being still so inaccessible to one another, so lacking talent and skill in human relations; while what we normally think of as conscious weighs with all but ineluctable weight on those fleeting, infinitely subtle, infinitely revealing images of the subconscious. Understood, these have it in them to illuminate, deeply to grasp, and finally to soothe a world; systematically ignored, to pile Pelion upon Ossa in mountains of fear and of tension that we can neither skirt nor scale.

Moreover, the premium we place on action has further undermined contact not only with others but, principally, with ourselves. Our most distinctive American philosophers, the pragmatists, found the test of truth in action. And in the pragmatic hierarchy action instruments thought; thought, by definition, deals only in the conscious. These two most powerful conscious drives surround as with an impregnable fortress the native, unpressured wisdom the subconscious holds for us, and it opens to no Ali Baba's password.

Inaccessible from without, the subconscious responds only to that inwardness, that spiritual holding of one's breath, that terribly elusive inner center, ineffably remote from thought and action.

67

These become powerful to the point of being self-evident as they build on those deeper insights of the subconscious which they alone can test and validate.

For we are a psycho-physical whole, which sometimes we appear to reckon with, more frequently to ignore. Thus we fragment ourselves; and we segregate ourselves alike from our living inner world and from our inanimate environment which initiates patterns that enter into life as well. Like variations on a theme in music, the more we know about these patterns, the more do we detect how they are repeated and modified, illuminating in the process what may yet be revealed as continuous progression from "primordial chaos" to the "noblest work of God."

The term *catalyst*, from chemistry, for example, suggests an obvious connotation in human relations, and a less obvious one: without apparent effort or observable change there are those in whose presence the harassed find peace, the turbulent, a measure of reasonableness, even the melancholy, hope.

But latterly biochemistry, by its refined methods, has revealed intense activity in the catalyst. And on such a comparably deeper psychological level is developed what appears as effortless skill in human intercourse: once we do succeed in penetrating to the subconscious, in understanding and interpreting it sincerely, it reflects and diagnoses our spiritual life for us, reacts to and on it as minutely, as unerringly, as the central nervous system on physical life. And vice versa. But having found the inside track to our own spiritual life, we have gone far toward understanding others'.

Our dreams, our fantasies, remain in form the same. We contravene the laws of space and time, of death and life, we exorcise ourselves, our friends, our foes, personify our fears, our passions. These sources of the tribal rites of times gone by, are today the minutest possible response to the epic of our lives, the microcosmic impact of events within our own electron orbit.

On those among us who are wise, psychological technique has thus bestowed well-nigh limitless expansion of experience. It embraces and reinterprets antiquity, the saga of the fundamental human adventure, as the eternal struggle emerges from the unrecorded, as myth, as poetry, as history—the boundaries shift with sharpening tools, and Agamemnon of the erstwhile myth emerges into the reality of an existing tomb, unmarred by time.

Knowledge has been said to be power, in the increasing control it supposedly gives us over nature and ourselves. But as the gap widens between knowledge and its responsible use—for most of us it remains just information—it may equally be said to leave us helpless. This is most often our confessed spiritual state, notwithstanding the potentially limitless rewards that await our responsible exploitation of the subconscious, in confidence and effectiveness, in personal freedom and the courage to conquer new worlds by understanding them.

6

BEING REGULAR

Mediocrity Becomes a National Aspiration

Max Wertheimer's was so basically an ethical nature that he considered ethics part of psychology. Certain it is that ethics remains, in some sense, actively indestructible, although it has been honored, with few exceptions, much more in the breach than in the observance throughout the millennia: there are few people—if any—without conscience functioning as guide or as guilt, in whatever ambience they may choose to deploy or to hide it.

At various times and places education has acknowledged ethics as character building. But automatically it has been segregated from the market place as education has for the most part been segregated from life, except when it is concerned with the application of special knowledge or skills. The continuity of the larger aspects of learning with living has come about, generally, only in higher adult education—in the individual case a purely voluntary outgrowth of current life interests and problems. These are broadened and deepened, often without the usual resistance, because of the insistence of life itself, which also tends to make them concrete and practical.

This happens especially in a culture such as ours, in which the emphasis is on action. Unless we "do something about it," nothing counts. At least, so it used to be. Action was the keynote and the pride of American culture, presumed good in itself. Winning independence, democracy, union, gave scope to statesmen and heroes. Exploiting the national wealth developed commercial genius, genially ruthless yet rarely ignoring completely or permanently the implicit debt to country and people.

We met war as a challenge, we have often failed to make the most of peace. Democracy today is given, or we think it is. "Nothing to *do* about it" but criticize. Mediocrity becomes a national aspiration. Again we call it "being regular"; except in open competition, it is bad taste to stand out among one's fellows.

The inventor, in this context, depends wholly on the sales manager; the designer errs at his cost. And, generally, success is measured by the mistakes one does not make.

Because thought has been discounted as inaction, we have not lived and grown in our great political tradition, nor yet created an embracing scientific one: at the highest point of psychological development we allay fear with suspicion, if we do not intensify it into panic and sadism; in a period of ultimate danger to the rights of man, a handful of heroic workers carry on and we manage a biennial government clash with the diehards.

The mood of the nation as a whole wavers between menace and inertia. We have loosed problems we tend to believe are beyond our strength, intensively and extensively. We recognize the intimate interdependence of all aspects of living and how ministering to one set of needs may badly tip the balance of another at least as important. A conference is called of the outstanding talent in every field to make the master plan for the U.S.A. in all departments.

"Not beyond?" thinking of our social, economic, and spiritual battlegrounds around the world whence immediate problems are pressing in upon us from all sides.

And the answer, "That would make it unmanageable."

Silently one reflects: Isn't it unmanageable as well on a national scale?

The mismanagement is borne in on us in so many fields of our contemporary endeavor: in a sense very different from the original, the right hand ignores what the left hand is doing, indeed the brain itself seems to be divided in much the same way, and subdivided. Although the contradictions we try to live have and will come up in a variety of connections, listing them briefly may serve to bring out how, necessarily, we destroy ourselves from within, destroy the individual potency which alone can make a world worth having and a life worth living: (1) Optimum and maximum are not synonymous, we have known now long and well, but size more than any other single feature is what advertising stresses. And in a kind of fairy-tale labyrinth we resell ourselves on size as if we had just discovered it, with a sixty-story Pan Am Building and a two-thousand-room Americana Hotel in the heart of New York City's most densely populated area. (2) The planners call for local centers of shopping and entertainment to avoid loss of time in traveling, to build up communities and neighborhoods. These very same planners, with Robert Moses as their standard-bearer, produce Lincoln Center and fight the battle for the crosstown elevated highway, which wipes out neighborhoods and makes new bottlenecks. (3) Machines that were meant to liberate us bind us: they must be kept busy twenty-four hours a day to repay the investment; nor can we afford disarmament for the same reason; again for the same reason crafts are obsolete, no matter what they may contribute by way of a superior product. (4) Television shares significantly in making creativity a slogan rather than an aspiration. Dean William Dunning of Columbia Engineering spoke with incisive critical eloquence on the Ford Foundation's six-million-dollar television project for science teaching. Not as spectacular, more astronomical in scale, are the man hours stolen from life by television programs that are for the most part less than indifferent. (5) Airline pilots with strictly limited working hours to keep them alert and active during flight, almost to a man take second jobs. (6) So do many schoolteachers for economic reasons, although they have trying work and long hours. We wail about the teacher shortage, yet the teacher's second job may as well be a waiter's as a teacher's. (7) The labor movement is looking for outside help to formulate new goals, recognizing that materially they have come to the end of the line; but where they go from here they have to find out from others, with the Electrical Union down to a twenty-hour week to insure maximum overtime. (8) In the academic world scholarship is measured by Ph.D.'s and pages of print, which may or may not be a measure of the intellectual life. (9) Efforts to prolong life proceed alongside continuing or increasing disparagement of the later years. (10) With the greatest emphasis on mental health, under which ethics is subsumed, the number of mental patients increases constantly and disproportionately. (11) Sportsmanship and sports, as we have seen, have less and less to do with each other. (12) With more and more public attention to the "population explosion," American marriages are younger than a generation ago, families notably and intentionally larger.

The foregoing is the briefest, quasi-random sampling of contradictions that are constant and insistent irritants in daily life. What emerges from it most prominently is that we are stuck fast in the clay of a materialistic universe. For such a limitation our gifts are excessive—what would become of birds so intent on their worms they forgot about flying?

We are compounding original sin. Having sold bliss for knowledge, knowledge has been traded for riches, riches for surfeit and confusion. In that progression the next step is plainly down and, very soon, annihilation. We bate our breath, and watch, and wait!

"How come?" runs the argot of the streets. "How come to us who stand for action and the young!" "Youth is the day of battle," from of old.

With our day the battle for spiritual life—nothing less. First poverty, then wealth gave center stage to the material. Under conditions far graver than we have ever known, the upward struggle must be joined again: the start this time is not from scratch but from an abyss of error deepened by vested interests. And the stakes? Civilization and the human soul.

Our operational means are in some ways superior if we choose to use them. Our schools as a civilizing force are by no means strictly local as they once were—through their student bodies they reach around the world. "Positively or negatively?" asks the cynic, and the answer is far from uniformly affirmative. Only in a moment of optimism might one indeed look upon our government's large-scale machinery for transnational learning as again on the threshold of adventure, and perhaps of hope; departure from the more usual phrase, *international education*, is to restore to the idea its full and pregnant meaning.

Interest focuses on the learning attitude— learning that, hopefully, may transcend not only national boundaries but one day even national self-interest and pseudo-self-interest. Contrast for a moment an Erasmus or a de Tocqueville with a Marco Polo or a Richard Halliburton. Such contrasts help us to remember that for the peace and advancement of the world we would often do better to stay at home than to go abroad in the conventional mood of the traveler, with unimagined possibilities for good, to be sure, but with far greater probabilities for evil.

Neither the ignorant, self-assured traveler—in these days increasing hugely the radius of his travel—nor the insecure, often isolated student is easily transformed into a source of international good will. And if the airplane and TV do tend to

make us all neighbors, it has been equally true—
from fairy tales to wars—that the hostility of
neighbors has been traditional, far more than their
friendship. In the One World which we predicate,
we have come to realize that the early evidence
shows little or no trace even of an approximation
toward understanding.

It begins to become clear, dazzlingly clear, that
education needs ethical values and seven-league
boots to catch up with other forms of communication, and that the fundamental problem of *international* education is to have the humility of true
learning overtake the arrogance of true national-
ism, which never appears in a purer strain than
when it finds itself "among foreigners."

That Frenchmen should be foolish enough to
call bread *pain*, when it is so obviously bread, is
irritating—not to say more—and in the spirit of
many of the things we feel called upon to correct.
The Chilean student in New York succumbs to
the boundless fascination of the U.S. and North
Americans; he is quite certain the same people do
not come to Chile. Which of us again has not felt
humiliated by fellow Americans, descanting loudly
on the virtues of America in some far-off city or
hamlet on the other side of the world!

We trained our minds to be conservative during
uncounted ages when culture struggled to be born.
We trained them to slow motion in the interests
of a laboriously developing civilization. Modern

science fundamentally altered the pace and our thinking has been left as hopelessly behind as Achilles actually left the tortoise. Nowhere do we feel that so acutely as in attempting to draw the consequences that flow from One World. It took thousands of years for men to feel themselves a nation. They want thousands more to feel themselves a world. But how many have they? Who would dare to say? Ethics today is self-preservation.

And humanity's fighting chance depends on its educators. Theirs is by definition the civilizing task. But the emphasis has been too exclusively intellectual—integrity has been seen as indispensable only to specific tasks, such as research and exams, not to the ordinary business of living. Hence it has not been a primary requirement of board members, faculty, or administrators. One is tempted to say it was taken for granted. To the extent that one would have *liked* to take it for granted, Wertheimer was right; but the record testifies to the opposite—with few exceptions humanity has lacked integrity through the ages, with no contrary distinction to be made for its intellectuals. All this evidence notwithstanding, we have done little or nothing since the days of the Ten Commandments and the Sermon on the Mount to promote the notion of necessary universality of the ethical life.

"Do as you would be done by" is the ethical

atom. Ralph T. Walker, internationally practicing architect, phrased it, "Selling is circular; not linear as we often think it is. We must develop the attitude in our students that would make for easier, readier contact with people of other nations, often very much lacking at international gatherings. We cannot sell ourselves to other people if we do not provide the opportunities by which they can sell themselves to us."

Balamu Jaberi Mukasa, premier of the African Kingdom of Bunyoro, recently visited this country to study education, race relations, and social welfare under the State Department's grant for "exchangees." With a B.A. from Morehouse College in Atlanta, and an M.A. from Yale, he had had his period of orientation in this country. *One, the Magazine for Christian Youth* wrote as follows with reference to his two weeks at St. Olaf College, Minnesota:

"A real highlight of Mr. Mukasa's visit came when he spoke . . . at the regular chapel service. The standing ovation given the premier brought tears to his eyes and indicated that students thought his was one of the most effective chapel talks they had heard.

"Al Jacobson, of Brooklyn, presented the visitor with a St. Olaf banner for his 11-year-old son. . . . More important though, is the 'John Hope Mukasa Scholarship,' which students and faculty members established to make it possible for the boy to attend St. Olaf some day."

Contrast with this the one-year scholarship of a young Indian girl at a large university, which was nearly exhausted in the process of orientation: "It was as difficult to find my way to what I needed and wanted as it would be for you if you were suddenly transplanted to India with no one really to help and advise when you got there."

In the large numbers of our foreign students we have a mutual opportunity of the greatest importance for ourselves and our visitors from abroad; but we have by no means used it as we might. In our One World, newly acquired, we have often sown rather than the seed the wind; and reaped the whirlwind.

It need not have been: some years ago students from India to Colombia, from the Gold Coast to Iceland, pooled their efforts and their talents in a delightful entertainment that produced a scholarship for a future student from overseas. With them we had the privilege of struggling through from argument to realization, from groping to goals that grew constantly clearer. We came to know at first hand the inspiring potentialities of being part of one of those international microcosms found in increasing numbers in America today. They are still far too few as compared with what could be.

The experience and its results, like so many others, suggest again the choice before us: that

81

One World at birth may live or die. Harmonious, interesting, intensely absorbing, if we can rise to life and its vicissitudes; but with the makings of a bigger Babel toppling to its destruction more surely if we shrink from the very range and magnificence of the opportunities which are implicit in being alive today.

What makes life good? Interest—adventure—accomplishment. But for how many are they within reach? The routine of one day follows the routine of another, precedes the routine of a third. In the factory, the office, the home, boredom and, with it, the sense of futility.

We owe it largely to the machine age. Feeding machines at work, being fed by them at play—instead of using them *we are being used by them increasingly*.

Adult education, viable at any level of culture, is the discovery or the rediscovery of ourselves, of our independent humanity, of leisure as a civilizing opportunity, not to prevent us from thinking but as an opportunity to contribute to it. "Ordinarily we are immersed in this sordid, sickening sea of business and most of our time is spent in talking shop and in other similar formal matters. The soul, however, needs some fare and it can only feed on what is congenial and wholesome," wrote the late Prime Minister Pant of United Provinces, India.

Adult education is the way back to one's own soul. And the life most meaningful to our individual selves, with all the variety that individualities require, may well prove a purposeful life for the community, the nation, the world. The apparently insurmountable roadblocks are the indifference, the accumulated individual incompetence and the resulting sordid sensuous negativism of our time. Instead of analyzing our own responsibility, we seem to see a solution in attacking others, as if we suffered less from the mistakes of others, which we cannot correct, than we do from our own, which we might!

But mutual vituperation engenders lasting resentments that drain energies, paralyze effort, and preclude enthusiasms. That we have the collective wisdom to solve our problems, if only we permitted it to operate individually, is something of which we are, generally speaking, unaware.

What adult education ideally gives to its votaries is direct contact with men and women chosen for their own efforts to add to the sum of knowledge, and the range of values—opportunity to see the human spirit at work, to see the imagination with which it conceives and formulates significant problems, the ingenuity with which it devises methods, the objectivity, the perseverance, the faith by which it finally arrives at solutions and puts them to use. Here is the dynamics of learning and living with the drama and the thrill of exploration, with the sense of fulfillment that flows from achievement and winning new areas from limitless reaches of the unknown.

Yet, prior to the opportunity for disinterested higher adult education, only the scholar or the professional was permitted the privilege of endlessly finding out. And only the Ph.D., with the requisite number of publications, could enjoy the luxury of sharing his inspiration with his fellows.

It is a truism to say that the more one knows the more one realizes how infinitesimal it is. The point is at least equally worth making that the more one finds out the more interesting life becomes, the more fascinating, and even, or perhaps especially, the more secure, i.e., spiritually secure, which is the only security that matters.

What do adult students of an adult school conceive as their task, their contribution in the 1960's? In 1980—in the twenty-first century—in that straining of humanity to be human that has gone on from prehistory, that we would like to believe will go on but for which right now we must entertain the very gravest doubts, our task is to find problems sufficiently near to us to make us interested, activities vital enough to make us generous, values significant enough to make us wise.

Tradition is what the past hands on to the future, forever in the making according to what we add to it or take away from it. We are heir to the quickening search for knowledge, the courage of spiritual adventure and planning, the conviction that the truth will make us free. As the century races toward its close, we confront a new deadline for acquiring the sense of responsibility by which freedom may achieve integrity and thereby redeem a world.

CHAPTER

7

MEANS FOR ENDS

Means Which We Have for Ends

Which We Have Lost from View,

Including That Ultimate End, the Human Soul.

And what it needs for its own happiness and growth." * What does it need? How long has it been since we asked ourselves? How long since anybody "regular" might legitimately ask, without forfeiting his "regularity"? How long, indeed, since we knew enough to ask? Knew that spiritual life was still the better part of life.

It was in that bygone age before Americans liked most to think of themselves as "realists," when the makers of America could, blushless, and for all to hear, utter what today is safe only on

* From a letter to Albert Mayer from the late Premier Pant of the United Provinces of India.

a postage stamp: "I have sworn hostility to every form of tyranny over the mind of man" (Thomas Jefferson). "Those who deny freedom to others deserve it not for themselves" (Abraham Lincoln).

To the rest of today's world we are not realists but materialists; the case could be made for idealists, were they not so hopelessly out of date. One actually stumbles over the word, suspecting in a moment of alarming insight that "suckers" may have replaced it.

Pure materialism is obviously a figment of the imagination. But of the nonmaterial we "realists" take account only when it is appropriately distorted, referring to every attempt at setting forth an idea as "selling," to every group of ideas as a "package," and this notwithstanding we have known, at least from Biblical times, "man cannot live by bread alone."

Our "friends" on this and other hemispheres have latterly come to dislike us as a nation. Our political wise men, our serious travelers, our Voice of America, have all found the reason—our propaganda is at fault. No one has thought of suggesting that it may be ourselves. And some go so far as to take that currently very fashionable position, "So what."

Realists like frankness and, frankly, we have earned dislike where we should have earned admiration, gratitude, even affection. We have tended constantly to brag about our material well-being in order to persuade ourselves that was all we needed or wanted—hardly the road to popularity in an 80 per cent undernourished world.

Even children outgrow the acquisitiveness of childhood; they get beyond collecting a new toy from every visitor. Not so with us Americans. With unswerving determination we follow the fashion whether in gadgets or the fine arts. And because we have glorified our materialism as realism, we have failed to see its shortcomings and its excesses.

Consider our technical gullibility, our readiness to believe in every mechanical device, actual or imagined. Contrast our intellectual, social and moral skepticism: thought is always suspect, sometimes, but only rarely, in good taste. A deadly quality of naïve sophistication, a bored restlessness are pervading.

This is the fate of the materialist; and the centripetal force developed has sucked countries and continents into our industrial-materialist orbit. The old spiritual cultures may conceivably survive; they cannot escape if we do not.

It is this all but hopeless tide in American and world affairs that we are fatefully called upon to turn, we who are striving to quicken the spiritual life and to feed the springs of creation—the only realistic way to turn the tide of destruction whether in the nation or the world.

America has more than its share of men and

women of primary spiritual interests and moral power for whom "the aristocracy of wealth has yielded to the aristocracy of service." As individuals they are recognized, often revered. Somehow they have not been a force in the total situation; they have had no voice in the collective voice of America, no organized personality. Perhaps that awaits the focalizing capacity of a network of adult schools of higher education, genuinely seeking to "educate" in its derivative sense, to consolidate our combined spiritual resources and render them indissoluble.

Basically the ethical, the intellectual, the artistic have a deep identity which may be destructive or constructive. The initial moment of accomplishment, of insight, or of genuine appreciation glows in any of these orders: in the thrill to a starlit sky; in the flash of a new connection between the known and the unknown; in a disinterested act of generosity.

Knowledge as understanding transforms, transposes, illumines, reflecting or refracting the light of any of the spiritual spectra even in trivial situations. A roomful of strangers is at first forbidding: as each gets his own identity, strain gives way to comradeship, to friendship, even to love. An island framed in a window, visited, became the cloistered courts of children in a home for orphans of the sailors of a great port city—then from the window it was seen with familiarity and warmth, with the

89

positively reinforcing connections of responsibility, knowledge, beauty.

But knowledge, even beauty, may also be destructive; any form of experience may vary in character and ultimate purpose *from understanding to possession*, from the joy of self-development and growth to the goad of self-seeking and power. Possession as possession, spiritual or material, is potentially divisive, almost inevitably. Power, or correlated forms of prestige, means power over others, directly or indirectly. The amount of it in the world is therefore necessarily limited. Automatically the assumption is that those who want it—and everyone is presumed to want it—must take it from those who have it. This is the implied origin of suspicion and jealousy, of fear, when these become so pervasive that they lose their specific object and frame of reference.

The votaries of knowledge and beauty may thus take two courses so wholly divergent that we refer to them as moral and immoral. One goes through self-aggrandizement to fear, if not to cruelty—as witness Cesare Borgia and other princes of the Renaissance or, in our day, that art and music lover Hermann Goering, and many of his fellow officers; the other through deeper and wider understanding to identification with larger and larger portions of mankind or indeed of life itself, like that other Renaissance prince, Francis of Assisi,

90

or our own contemporaries, Einstein and Schweitzer.

Such contrasts—less extreme, to be sure, and less dramatic—with qualifications and exceptions, are inherent in our workaday world. The power-seekers are all around us, awaiting their chance or grasping it. Again the Midas touch makes material even the immaterial; while by a reverse conversion process spiritual forces tend to infuse what is material, in those from whom essential humanity alienates the basic position of power.

So it was on a late afternoon in early March, when winter for a day had yielded to spring, that a moment of overwhelming beauty prompted the insistent question, "In what sense is beauty, meaning?" A slanting beam of the sun on sprays of rose-colored French heather had made them suddenly luminous against their shadow on a pale gray wall. Deep stillness grew alive with beauty as the day's end recalled the season's beginning, and evoked a strangely clear conviction of knowing the meaning of life.

At one time or another all of us have said that life had no meaning. Except as an article of faith, few of us have said the opposite. And yet, when by the bad luck of impaired brain capacity, we are called upon to function on fragments of mind, we cease entirely to function if meaning goes out. In the jargon of the day, meaning and distinctively

91

human life are synonymous on the operational level—not to say more.

Meaning is defined in terms both of truth and of value, of knowledge and aim. It is integral in the ethical as in the intellectual order, and on the bedrock of harmony it sinks a common foundation. Truth builds and rebuilds the structure of knowledge to take account of unreconciled facts—the law of contradiction is the first law of logic—while persistent conflict, whether in goals or in values, undermines institutions and men.

But harmony belongs first to beauty.

Antithetical to it except as transitional, are discord, contradiction, conflict, in a word, destruction. So it is that deviation from beauty and truth becomes sin, an offense against the moral order; and value at its peak is three-dimensional. The great scientist has a powerful aesthetic motive and scrupulous honesty is the heart of his method. The distinction of the artist turns on his sincerity and the universality of his conceptions as much as on his purely artistic gifts. Art, moreover, generally pioneers social change, the ceaseless reorientation of existence on changeless foundations.

One reflects on more essential, more prolonged and complex experience, e.g., the day-to-day life of a very young girl and how it became part of the inheritance of the Western world: *The Diary of Anne Frank* played simultaneously in twelve German theaters. It was received in silence; for the first time, the ultimate, individual tragedies of the campaign to exterminate the Jews came home to the German people. Art succeeded where knowledge had failed.

On Anne Frank life had made its impact to the point where she could no longer absorb, she had to understand. And in the process she made others understand.

By any human scale and in every dimension the panorama of events is endless; therefore, formless. Experience must be "disciplined" by science or "formed" by art before it can have "meaning," be used in other than the elemental or the more complicated reflexes of self-preservation. The successive steps are selective, structural, significant, aesthetic in an ascending progression. But science in the long view is open-ended and cumulative, tending toward unity. Art deals in wholes of its own making, each in itself complete. In direction and emphasis, with an aesthetic component in common, science further relates to art as measurement to evaluation, discovery to creation, discipline to freedom, law to form.

It follows that only science is susceptible of proof. Yet neither may art violate experience, on which it is the searching, seeking commentary— penetrating the present, adumbrating a changing future, focusing and weighting meaning, the Geiger counter of Eternity.

Under Aristotle's influence we have thought of

form and substance in separate categories. When we practice art, or genuinely experience it, perfection is reached when form and substance are indissoluble, when art has found conviction, conviction art. This indeed is how, as artists, we become subjectively aware, spiritually completely certain that we have achieved what we meant to achieve; in this sense art is value, the sublimation of life.

To Aristotle the art of tragedy was purging— "through pity and terror." So is all art, through the basic understanding, spiritual and emotional, from which it flows and which, when it is most compelling, it transmits. By us as creators the process is more deeply, because actually, experienced. We approach it the more nearly in the art of others according to the measure of greatness of their art, the range and the insight of our experience.

A deeply stirring event brings to consciousness some surpassing line of poetry, all but forgotten, and understanding becomes more profound, incisive, lasting. This very knowing use of words is art in its most prevailing and essential aspect. It represents the need to write, and all that is implicit in it—to think, to feel, to "compose," to articulate. From thinking we have so long estopped ourselves that we fail to recognize its deep necessity as a source of restorative, regenerative power. Sustained thinking demands writing—beyond a given point the mind neither formulates nor retains, precisely, the successive steps, the multiple considerations that lead to or reinforce conclusions, that make at once for comprehensiveness, penetration, validity, conviction. But in time the author craves the completing auditor for whom to re-create experience with its most telling impact.

Style, form may or may not at first be in the purview of the writer. Indeed it may never be. But this is to deny perhaps our most significantly human potential. Form is a universal aspect of creation on any level, words the human means most widely used. For those who feel no urgent call to work with other materials—even for many who do —words are the medium par excellence in which to develop form.

Life is the struggle for order, for form. The Genesis story recognized it as incompatible with material or spiritual chaos. Order indeed preceded life, the life struggle is to maintain or enhance it. Words, language as humanity's spiritual exchange medium, have endless and repeated capacity for the ugliness and the frustration of insensitivity, ignorance, deception, in short for chaos. Or for beauty, according to the gold reserve of thought that makes their value, and the unremitting effort to fit thought and words exactly as it were, inevitably; then curiously, and without seeking it, but commensurately with the success of that effort, there is unmistakable style, artistic creation. The subjective purging effect comes by way of order in the mind where order is needed most.

Conversely, deliberately to exploit words for other purposes, thus to obscure and confuse meaning, becomes the basic crime against mankind spiritually conceived. It ranges from the exploitation of dictators and would-be dictators to much of the language of advertising and what is known as promotion: "Christmas Sale-A-Thon," "Briar Brown, a new interpretation that accents the male look," "The wonderful world of WCBS," "Great giftsmanship: sweaters for all men" (from a cursory look at a Sunday *Times*).

"To be confused" is both one of the time's major clichés and one of its major actualities. Yet we deliberately confound confusion by gross abuse and overuse of language, medium for advancing experience from philosophy to poetry and intellect to passion. The other side of the balance is weighted by those who underuse it. From the pace of the working day in a mechanized world they seek to recover by more mechanization. Their relaxation is television, which permits them to doze; their adventure is speed, which allows them to risk; the relative facility of throwing switches fills even the interstices of daily living left from the described pursuit of the repair services that climax built-in obsolescence, bureaucracy, and frustration.

TIME AND HISTORY

The Unremitting Struggle for Yet Another Start

A student neither of history nor of art, yet passionately wedded to European culture like numberless of my contemporaries, for me the question arises why living in history generates the purest serenity, why the affinity for it is deeply instinctive, what makes it a vital source of spiritual nourishment and strength. . . .

The deepest instinct of the living is the sense of kinship with one's own, the species recognizing itself in any or all of its exemplars, in what they do and what they leave behind them.

Perhaps in the last analysis this is the true meaning of history.

We are not historically minded for the most part. We have lived and practiced and carried with us that most distinctive part of our historical legacy, political and social freedom, so bred in the bone we didn't have to study it, neither in its origins nor in its development.

Our culture as music and the fine arts is relatively new.

The genius of our material culture has been the working conviction that each age demands its own characteristic embodiment as of right, to the exclusion, hence often the annihilation, of what has preceded.

Thus briefly may we account for our lacking as a people any recognized sense of history.

"Recognized," because basically perhaps the lack of a sense of history is impossible. That would mean denying the instinct of the species for itself and its works. But this happens only when we are "studying" history, not when we are living it, as we do in Europe. The Swiss Alps, humanized by their little villages, their tinkling herds, their rock-hung chalets, strike a deeper chord than the utter wilderness of the Andes or the Rockies. This is history, man's hand and record at its simplest. It is the foundation of what draws us irresistibly, with or without more detailed knowledge, toward our own past when we can have that completing experience of living with it and in it.

As Europe—and through it our cultural foundations—grows closer physically and spiritually, as Fulbrights grow more numerous and tourists more receptive, as spanning the ocean becomes still less formidable, we may wake one day to yet another concomitant phenomenon, the sense of history.

I am reminded of a tablet at San Gimignano. It marks the room in which Dante as ambassador from Florence pleaded his cause some seven centuries ago. Thousands of nameless contemporaries made their cold or impassioned pleas in other rooms long vanished, long replaced, or failed to make them. Today's Dante, if there is one, stands in the same relation to posterity of the twenty-seventh century as do we, his contemporaries, endlessly absorbed into history.

What sounds like a platitude is an arresting fact in the stream of human life as one tries to get clear just how one relates to past and to future. Straining to look deeper in either direction, to see farther and more clearly, one reflects with René Dubos that "biological and social history provide well-documented situations in which the changes in the environment have been so sudden as to prevent the successful operation of adaptive processes. It is in this context that one must consider the unforeseeable consequences for man of the changes which presently occur in his environment at an accelerated rate and in uncharted directions."

In this panorama of change, as we watch it today, specialization accounts for a large area and a long perspective. Founded, to be sure, on results of basic research, the limited, sharply defined investigation, the close analysis, have borne fruit in important inventions and discoveries, from electronic brains to polio serum. The problem of meaning raised by them, namely the relation of these discoveries to people—in the continuum, history—is chiefly the problem of a new integration or, at the very least, no deterioration of the old.

A recent conference bore directly on these thoughts. It was called by the Academy of Medicine to discuss the role of the family in mental health. All the delegates were from health agencies combating single illnesses. They were trying to puzzle out what might be done to involve the family as significantly responsible for the patient's ill- or well-being. But the job of each was special, care of tubercular or heart sufferers, and the family was just none of their business. In India, on the other hand, or in Lambaréné, in any relatively "primitive" community, a patient doesn't go to a hospital unaccompanied by his family. One is reminded of the fairy's gift of the three wishes, used up to regain the *status quo ante*. Or as Alvin Johnson once said, "It takes a hell of a lot of psychology to get back to common sense."

We have long told ourselves that the sanction of time and antiquity is not necessarily a measure of value. But neither is it a measure of foolishness. The closest scrutiny is in order before we use major force to wrest time-honored practices from tradition and discard them, then marshal even greater effort to restore them. This is not to men-

100

tion all that, through the ages, we have hopelessly shattered. Currently our mechanized culture has for many of us made it a project and a luxury to use our hands; a harmless illness, averted in childhood, has lethal potential in the later years.

In other situations we are stymied, held suspended, as to what may prove to be the reconciliation of the wave and the particle theory of light, of the very law of contradiction itself. Modern art is thought by one philosopher to point the direction in its arresting, consciously difficult, multiple perspectives, achieving a precarious moment of unity, rather than the eternity we once pursued— the first considered, well-thought-out possibility for living not merely dangerously, as today we must, but creatively as well—the challenging hypothesis to which to relate a future. It need not be to foreclose a dawn on yet another period of stability at some distant day, but our day is one of changes so momentous that unity, it must be recognized, can be no more than a stepwise progression.

It makes the image of the new era almost blindingly clear, with confidence radiating from such resources of courage and comprehension as we tap only in situations we account extreme. Until then we try and try, and try again, to make pygmies stand in for giants, with elevator heels, seniority rights, and a television set. What we are doing is to make our horizons wider, our worlds more adventurous, at least by implication, our people narrower, smaller, weaker—two lines that from a point of common origin diverge toward infinity.

It is our task, as it is the task of every generation, to distinguish between acceleration and progress, momentum and creation. But such is the contemporary rate of acceleration, such the difficulty of creation in given conditions, that it takes primordial strength to brake the one, achieve the other. If we fail, we pay the price of history's final and its costliest lesson, annihilation of what we have created—a price paid by every earlier culture that history records. If we succeed, we reap its greatest reward in the hardest and purest act of creation, predicated as it is on vistas too vast yet to be discerned or even clearly conceived.

"Slowly, slowly, patiently" (as the nurse said to the infant) vistas may transmute into visions as mists precipitate into streams, experience draining into the watersheds of ideas—what of subwholes and of history life has yielded to contemplation in the unremitting struggle for yet another start.

A sensuous revelation; the questions raised by uncritical affirmation or denial of the contribution of others; knowledge as extensive and intensive, and the relation of each to the other—such were the elements in what follows:

A thing of beauty intensifies its beauty when

it is affirmed in another context. A burnished red camellia, handed to the wearer of a red and ochre scarf, was enhanced to the point of solemnity, passed from the purely aesthetic into the realm of thought and of value as something ultimately, eternally right!

Perhaps this is how the particular, when we experience it directly, irresistibly suggests its own universality.

An affirmation just as profoundly true, when it is another's, may be unconditionally accepted or resisted, on the nature less of the facts than of personal reaction to them. And again human life and its progress are predicated on the experience of others, on accomplishments of our contemporaries and our forebears in the never-ending rethinking of history.

Subjective and objective considerations may alike be construed as enlargement or abridgment of self, real or supposed. Personality determines what constitutes either: being reasonable or stubborn, discriminating or gullible, imaginative or literal, steady or wavering.

So do we let survival depend on our personal whims, our capacities or our lack of them—survival, and the depths of experience, living of the kind, when we permit it, that tells us unequivocally, "It is well worth our while." For it is as experience accumulates that it becomes many-sided, subtle, meaningful to the point of ideas;

ideas, as they accumulate, are organized, then generalized in a life, a generation of lives, many generations of lives, disclose to the race its significance.

Communication, public relations, semantics, symbolism, words at once glib and complex, tend both to emphasize and to obscure the real meaning for civilization, for culture, and for individual life of the reception and transmission of experience, genuinely assimilated from other people, other lands, other times:

> *Scattered, unsure beginnings*
> *May combine in direction, and flow*
> *With contours growing constantly clearer*
> *As a river, nearing the sea;*
>
> *Or if the streams fail to merge*
> *And each goes its own separate way,*
> *They never do reach the sea—*
> *Dry beds disappear in dry sands.*
>
> *Flood tide of the wisdom of age,*
> *Or its parching, withering drought,*
> *In each of our lives, or in all.*

Envoi: the contradiction that is America. In this metropolis of New York, once made up residentially—within the memory of half its population—of something like 99.9 per cent brownstones for its middle-class dwellings, as only an American-English city could be, an original brownstone has become all but extinct. Recently I was invited to visit a dwelling, unique since 1900 for having been constructed on empty land! The more or less Victorian granite fronts of the multi-storied, still entirely serviceable buildings, of the last half century are rapidly disappearing in favor of the "functional" glass towers of today. Conservation even of the White House façade required dedicated and well-organized private effort! And we are a nation of antique hunters.

Notwithstanding plowing under, farm and export subsidies, no economist has yet dared to promulgate any other economic theory for America than the gospel of the expanding economy on whatever terms of destruction: nor has any economist attempted sensibly to implement this theory whether with a practical plan of distribution, or with a different way of spending the national income. Both are too radical to be considered worthy of attention, much less of study. The psychology of waste has been deliberately promoted as prestige, if not as virtue; selling is reinforced by advertising as basically far more important than production technique, top soil for growing presidents and board chairmen. Industry's newest golden rule follows naturally: material obsolescence built in, from hosiery to washing machines, social obsolescence inherent in anything other than the latest model.

But our immediate concern is not with economics. It is with history, with wiping out the past

105

so far as the material record is an important part of it. One wonders, for example, what prompted the restoration of Williamsburg while Chestnut Street in Salem, and the three or four other remaining streets like it in the United States, probably require just a local real-estate boom to deliver them to the sledgehammer and the blast. Is it the need and the merit of always "doing" something, emphasis on creating, so-called, rather than on the much less spectacular, less advertisable virtue of conserving? This is for the most part unintelligible to Americans if they can afford the luxury of replacing. A small Greek lady of my acquaintance, aged eighty-two, who knows how to restore everything from rare point lace to heavy, metal-embroidered velours in their fourth score of years, conserves the beauty of these objects with an emotion akin to pure joy. It is an area we do not know.

The potency of profit for profit's sake, matched by the preoccupation with "the American standard of living" and longer hours of the leisure we don't know how to use, has left no room for the more essential satisfactions, for perspectives more distant than the economic, for creating the physical-spiritual environment in America we seek in other parts of the world. Whether we know it or not— and the fewest of us do—we miss the visible, tangible legacy of those who have preceded us. It is indispensable to the sense of life's completeness, hence to its intelligibility and its calm.

A new fashion has taken social possession: we appear to be starting on American "lines of succession"—currently John Doe IV—formerly reserved for the direct line of descent in a reigning house. It is one of those final characteristic and slightly ridiculous contradictions, a kind of snobbish and trivial projection into the future of the history we seem to prefer to ignore in the past.

9

"THE CREDITOR NATION"
AND THE SUMMONS

To Make of Us Who Dwell in America

Americans Worthy of Their Trust

In the postwar wave of know-nothingism, preceding the Hungarian revolt against Russia, refugees were often thought of as polluting that "pure American" strain distinguished chiefly by its bigotry. To one who has had the good fortune to live with the élite of European immigration, to be in contact with some of the small band of their like-minded contemporaries surviving abroad, to renew familiarity with the art and the architecture that cannot be re-created, the notion of the United States as being entirely on the giving end requires revision.

Although we plead guilty as a people to lacking the sense of history, it is a matter of common experience that, like wine, virtue—whether of heart, brain, or character, of people or things—needs time to reach its fullest development, each in its own period. Moreover, that "no man is an island" in time or in space, and much less so today than when Donne first found his moving formulation.

We seem often to confuse individuality with individualism, community with conformism; we often overlook that characteristic feature of values and of knowledge that tends to make them cumulative in national as in personal life, vertically and horizontally.

From NATO and the Peace Corps back to Point Four and Lend Lease, we have stressed mutual security, technical assistance, economic cooperation. Envoys and Congressional committees have now and again reproached the NATO countries for not pushing to rearm in the face of our generosity. Periodically we have "gotten tough": "On X divisions at a particular nation's expense depends our offer of Y." The simple justice of self-help on the basis of help from others, the simple laws of proportion, make up the simple Congressional view of life.

Battlefields of two wars, graves of unnumbered civilians, huge ratios of loss to population and wealth, migrations, refugees, concentration camps, planetary dispersal of families, the profound weariness of war—and total war means total weariness—these factors in Western Europe's reluctance to take the brunt of rearming some of us have understood, more of us have not.

None of us has understood adequately the meaning of Western Europe to the Western world: it has meant continuity, to speak personally, our cultural inheritance, the almost physiological experience of being heir to the ages. Only late, suddenly and accidentally, unerringly and overwhelmingly, there stood forth on the rugged slopes of Greece, in the columns of its temples, in its stadia, its theatres and its stoas, the living germ of Western culture, of democracy and freedom—individual humanity in its moment of birth. And in a flash one knew that protecting Western Europe was protecting not our own front line but our deepest selves, our creations in art, ideas, and institutions.

That individual physical development approximates development of the species came to us via the insights of biological evolution. Psychoanalysis uncovered spiritual evolution, the psychological role of the historic past in the present and for the future—source of that American way of life which is deep in the national tradition, deeper in the individual soul. The question formulates itself, as the archaeologists excavate, "Did successive civilizations go to their doom because men were defeated in war, or did men suffer defeat because their heritage had lost its meaning?"

To weaken in any part that laboriously built structure known as Western civilization is to start certain collapse of the whole—to abandon any form of help to Western Europe would be once again to make the costly discovery that money is far cheaper than what through the ages it has helped to build.

Yet have we been only too ready to ask, "If they [the refugees] don't like it, why don't they go back where they come from?" Rarely, "What can we do to make them happier?" And even though psychology comes close to being a national religion, with growth its creed.

Why again do we pay substantially for an imported product, while the American abroad feels obliged to tell any and every captive audience "how we do things in America!"

Blithely and mutually exclusive, ideas and actions—or just different ideas—often have each their own worlds. The *cordon sanitaire* established between them was a device of the age of Puritanism to make life acceptable at once to man and to a punishing God. The Deity of today is kindlier, Himself distrustful of punishment, but our inheritance remains to be remade in this new image of our God.

Fortes fortuna adiuvat—fortune favors the brave.

So might we epitomize the great moments in American history, or any history. To seize the critical moment is to understand or at least to sense

111

its total significance.

Once again today the historical process has shown us of the United States arresting signs of its favor. Alone among the world's great nations and more of the smaller ones, the mass tragedy of the times, genocide and the enslavement of peoples, has unrolled before the eyes of a single American generation still in its prime, without major injury to its wealth or its power.

We see ourselves the Chosen People of the Twentieth Century. Risen to greatness out of the European melting pot and the American opportunity, we fell into the petty ways of exclusion, and have had greatness again thrust upon us: international leadership with new human resources of mind, character, and skill from the six continents and the seven seas, at the cost of shattering breaks with people, tradition, and lifetime achievement, the deep inhumanities of troubled and fearful times, the stubborn resistances of utterly new and unknown worlds.

To ourselves and to these, the wiser survivors of the streamlined tyrannies of the twentieth century, we the people owe a debt that can be neither forgiven nor funded because the stake is civilization itself. It is our third and our crucial historic mission. We will have no other if we fail.

Thus conscious of ourselves as Americans we came uniquely to incorporate into everyday language the expression "un-American." Our neighbors had not thought of the un-South American, European nations of the un-French, un-Dutch: national loss of a sense of humor is a serious matter. With it goes loss of perspective, which is the basis of sanity.

And while subversion has lost the front page, the spiritual illness it represents lurks where it is perhaps more dangerous for not being on the front page, in the sanctions of government, e.g., that have referred to some prospective immigrant as "on parole," in an attempt—often unsuccessful— to drive him back even after the superhuman effort of getting here; that withhold the right to travel from some individuals and in some countries; in the sanctions both of government and industry that blacklist and blight uncounted of our citizens; that make for a way of life lacking in sensitivity and in courage while gradually, through the support we give it, the unspeakable becomes the everyday. We hunt security risks instead of witches, seek the reasons for them and the remedies not where they are, but in a variety of devices that permit us to avoid our clear responsibility.

Every difficulty, physical or psychological, focuses on the weakest organ—the dyspeptic gets indigestion equally from food or poor business, and to those susceptible, headaches may come from eye strain or a family row. The national headache has been known interchangeably—or successively—as un-American, subversive, Communist, fellow traveling, with this difference: that Communism is the real national weakness only insofar as it has become the chosen form of national hypochondria. Its phases range from purveying information to the Soviets to having a remote relative whose wife belonged to the Southern Conference for Human Welfare or even read Karl Marx.

Some bright mind discovered that it was hard for a teacher to show up the weaknesses of Communism if it was subversive to know anything about it. This is not the only dilemma for the American who doesn't want to be subversive; to denounce and to spy is not subversive, not even to subject to "ordeal by slander," but beware of standing up for your friends! Your principles. Your faith in the free institutions of your fathers.

How did we get into such unholy confusion? And how can we get out of it? If we must use the terms, what is it that *American* stands for—has stood for—to make this country America? And what has done so much violence to it as to deserve to be called subversive or un-American?

Let us begin with *The New York Times* of a particular morning some years ago: "An invitation to Dr. Kirtley F. Mather of Harvard University, President of the American Association for the Advancement of Science, to address a student 'brotherhood banquet' Sunday night was withdrawn today by the chaplains of Syracuse University. . . .

" 'In the interest of our fellowship of unity,' explained the Reverend Dr. Charles Noble, head of the university staff of chaplains, and 'because of Dr. Mather's previous and present relationship with certain organizations listed by the Attorney General's office as objectionable.'

" 'The university itself is not backing down on the issue of free inquiry and academic freedom,' he added. 'As a token of its good faith the dean has invited Dr. Mather to deliver the [Protestant] sermon Monday.' "

Which of these actions is American? Which subversive or un-American?

Can we only deplore the inquisitors and the tribe they have borne? Bow to the least and the meanest of them? Rely on time to kill or cure?

Or does it behoove us to remember, to say to ourselves again and yet again, "The secret of happiness is freedom and the secret of freedom is courage"?

The Llaneros of Colombia, recently visited, are a lesson in courage, conscious of their lacks, conscious of their values. They have emerged from years of the struggle against dictatorship and violence with large mortality, displacement of population, lawlessness, poverty, and nearly 50 per cent illiteracy—determined for democracy and order.

115

For a moment I felt part of it on the Llanos Orientales, where the days are tropical with sounds and the pitiless, still intensity of the sun; the nights with stars, deep silence, and softly moving air that restores tranquillity—unless laden, as it often is, with *sancudos*, the malarial mosquitoes that penetrate all the clothing one can tolerate.

The dust and the mud are beyond the imagining of a North American city dweller, and each and every day concludes with full-scale "personal spring cleaning" that makes concretely vivid the ongoing quality of man's battle with nature at large, and with his own.

But night begins at six near the equator and in the widely scattered *fincas* there is no light. Time then for thought, for the physical to become spiritual, it may be in the manner of that unspectacular penetration of water through soil, of the leap through space of an electric charge, of the force exerted by the magnetic field of an idea.

Situation and process crystallize in this transformation of the day's events into thought: exchange of reality for neurosis and vice versa; amount and intensity of ill or well-being on earth; motive, range, and point of termination of concern for others, the area of indifference or of callousness induced by necessity; the rise and fall of cultures; the old experience, the new knowledge, and the extreme difficulty of learning from either.

W. O. Galbraith, B.B.C. representative in Colombia, Ecuador and Venezuela from 1945 to 1949, writes, "Above all things the Colombian is a great friend. . . . Associated with his capacity for friendship is his warm generosity. . . ." Drawing on elemental psychological considerations, one might infer that a relatively closed society, in constant and immediate confrontation with forces that might destroy it, had spontaneously come upon friendship at once as its reward and its simplest, most potent weapon, without being closed to the contribution of law, of education, of material culture. These are all good in themselves, but experience none the less seems to suggest that they often weaken men's basic bonds.

Currently these are strong on the Llanos, alike beyond the range of North Star and Southern Cross. Yet inevitably one asks, Will they survive under higher levels of physical well-being or, generally, is some form of necessity basic to humanity's apparently most disinterested loyalties that are warp and woof of the social fabric, realization in depth that no man is an island?

Take in this context our government and people in 1954. The Attorney General made two important contributions to statesmanship. The first was to provide "one [spy] case after another" for party worthies "to hang on the Democrats from now until next November." The second proposed, in order to make good on the promise, to legalize the submission in federal courts of evidence obtained

117

from wiretapping; and to grant immunity to informers, to the world's Bentleys, its Budenzes and Chamberses.

The Attorney General's is one of the oldest Cabinet positions, created with the most far-reaching responsibility for the future in law of the country itself. Not for the last six months of a four-year administration, but as needed, its announced program was to furnish muck for the muckrakers by making a nation of betrayers and betrayed.

Mr. Velde, emerging from a Congressional conference at the White House, found the discussion "very congenial," he told newsmen. The late Senator McCarthy was "not displeased at anything he heard." Thus did both lawmakers show their usual objectivity in stating their criteria of government.

The unprepared reader, opening his Sunday paper, felt a thrust to the heart of the nation and to the hearts that make the nation. Of a sudden, and decisively, he became responsible custodian of nearly two centuries of inherited, at times embattled freedom, felt the tug at the deepest strands of personal patriotism, knew in the very marrow of his bones—perhaps for the first time—the meaning of tradition and of the American role in history: "they have rights who dare maintain them —and an instinct bears along round the earth's electric circle the swift flash of right or wrong."

118

May the Divinity that shapes our ends by its own dialectic help us to draw strength from the depths to scale the heights, and make of us who dwell in America Americans worthy of their trust.

CHAPTER

10

FRIENDSHIP

Only the Untrammeled Spirit

Attains to the Summits

Friendship Is One of Them, Embracing Humanity

The institutions of mass production and bureaucracy, "the American standard of living," the progeny of all these, all interconnected, relate in some ways to the subtleties and refinements of living as did mastodons and mammal herds to the unseen world of the micro-organisms: quite simply, the existence of that world was unknown. But the tremendous disparity in size is not indicative of disparity in positive significance, still less of generic survival capacity unless in inverse ratio.

The progressive dehumanization of our culture seems to correlate with size; the light-years elude the layman's grasp, and so humanity's consciousness, to a greater extent than do the atomic nuclei. Magnification brings the ineffably small within our range; no inverse process has been found to apply to the ineffably large, minimally accessible to observation, which is extended by reason and imagination.

The force of logic, moreover, carries us on to larger and larger units of investigation as inevitably as the waves from a common center. But living in a world in which theory underlies practice, and practice must corroborate theory, the inevitability of practical decisions has to be reckoned with as well, although it is of a different order from the inevitability of theory. There is, in fact, no part of the real world, computers notwithstanding, in which limits have not to be prescribed— *real* is used here as synonymous with effectively operable—and optimum size, which may be small, medium, or large, is at least a familiar concept, as pointed out repeatedly. Nevertheless, the emotional appeal of the vast, along with its "logical necessity," remains potent despite the difficulties it is bound to generate.

One unexpected and far-reaching result, among others, is that the computer has become not merely the key to the universe but, to some minds, its creator; from which it has followed that statistics are thought to exhaust its secrets. Except in France, where a kind of ultimate intellectual clarity and skepticism combine to transcend even the mathematical as all-inclusive; the computer was rejected there until it was literally imposed on the French by I.B.M.

With the progressive fascination of the large, we have seen the need to step up the scale—extensively speaking—of our own interests and accomplishments, to the necessary exclusion of intensity, at times, thus compounding a fallacy in at least two directions. For on size we are beaten before we start; as the frame of reference grows, so does recklessness or the sense of helplessness—one often leads into the other; and abandoning intensity, we have abandoned the possibility of mastery, with it even the sense of mastery for, humanly speaking, mastery cannot be divorced from intensity.

But remembering, in however garbled a way, that we are human, we pay garbled human tribute, again in that well-known and all-embracing contemporary phenomenon, public relations. These tributes range from a wide variety of social activities to using selections from the classics as advertising material. This seems, in fact, to be the one recognized way of giving the classics wider currency, concealing under an acceptable business caption the appearance of any depth of sentiment or of understanding. Having thus concealed it, we rediscover certain basic values when they have all but vanished—the unseen because unseeable, the spiritual.

In this particular sphere of activity—and in twentieth-century New York, except for watching television, everything is activity—of intertwining public and social and human relations, the cocktail party is the great contemporary phenomenon. It is distinguished by numbers, by the complete impossibility of speaking seriously to anyone, and by the available liquor which further guarantees the level of conversation. Where fewer people assemble, there are always the card games, the night clubs, athletics as performance or conversation, social, professional, or business gossip.

But living has likewise its spiritual laws of self-preservation, aware that humanity's outstanding characteristic is not knowing when to stop in a direction taken, or even that one can stop. Unused areas of heart and brain begin to stir in memory —real or symbolic—of those perfect archetypes, preserved, according to Plato, from the recollections of another world. Whence but from there, in these contentions, often superficial, materialistic times, could we take the need for friendship and the seed, the amenities of genuine social intercourse based on the deeper preoccupation with life?

For our society, despite its conformism or because of it, or both, is disintegrating in families and communities and associations, above all in the individual, personal standards on which these groupings rest. The core of renewal is in these standards, and the hope in these first stirrings, perishable, and promising, and profound. They appear in small gatherings of genuinely congenial people to whom "common interests" in the narrow sense are neither essential nor necessarily relevant; yet with such a tangible sense of well-being in each other's presence that one feels constrained to become clear as to what makes it.

Sincerity is its foundation—there is no real well-being without it. In concrete manifestations, always easier to deal with, it is of a piece with honesty. Two recent incidents—the simplest—showed the extent to which it is currently exceptional, one in a West Side market, the other in a high-level Fifth Avenue bookshop. In both cases it involved a purchaser, pointing out to personnel financial errors against themselves—about four dollars in the bookshop, less than a third of that in the market. It was embarrassing to note the manifest surprise and gratitude in each case, for being able to count on the genuine reliability even of a customer!

Within an atmosphere of mutual trust, a serious and congenial group is moved to examine life experience, what it has been in each case, what each has been able to make of it. This exchange may be on the plane of adventure, it may be the result of a profoundly explored idea, the discussion may be of similar or divergent events, real contact in the group emanates a sense of companionship, humanly distinctive, gratifying, even exalting. A comparable intellectual level, high-caliber humor and vitality enhance it.

One is on the way to friendship, embracing those wide variations in genuine human relationship, intimate, sometimes intense, that promise a "God in His Heaven, all's right with the world." No disparity matters, of age, nationality, occupation, race or religion or culture—it is a treasure available at will, a conscious possession, however rarely it may be called upon.

The range in a given circle of friends is down from ninety-two: the most interesting evening in the life of a young man of nineteen was, in his own statement, the one spent with later-than-middle-aged scientists. One of an oppressed minority, starting his fifth decade, sought advice in the group on returning to his home country. A prominent member of a government in exile took counsel with a member of the circle on a personal political decision. A young matron preferred these "different-age parties" to those of her own contemporaries. A talented college senior sought more frequent contact with close-to-a-septuagenarian. Each of these statements is the tiniest segment of the warp and woof of the spiritual ties that bind us. Behind each is a "case history." Case histories that together contribute significantly to the reach and the deepening content of a life.

A life that, on the whole, carries or is carried,

that bears or is borne. If the former, there is no end except the end of life to the number of those to whom one can lend a moment of strength. Sometimes this is reciprocal, but mankind on the whole is comprised of those who help and those who are helped. Individual emphasis tends to go one way or the other, although not exclusively; one can exist even less perhaps on unmixed receiving than on unmixed giving.

As one travels over the world and comes momentarily closer to new nationals and their problems, one is suddenly overwhelmed as by a tidal wave, thinking of the many human destinies one touches more closely! Yet so transiently. And those, innumerable, one never touches—the Greek tragedies, the treadmills, the farces, the adventures, the triumphs, the trivia. Where and why does human kinship stop? And the answer, "Where it can go no farther."

Only in the last decade, to look back for a moment, did we in America discover ourselves to be overspecialized. Prominent technical schools throughout the country reorganized their courses of study to include more of the humanities: the specialist was bound to be superior who was well-grounded in them, whether he was lawyer, physician, or engineer. But the pendulum, as usual, was not regulated for the median arc, and swung from excessive specialization toward such inclusiveness as we are still enlarging, although we are unequipped to deal with it productively. We confront inescapably that recurrent need for the basic decision—Lewis Mumford referred to it recently as "human intervention in 'The System' ": when is a change due and how far does it go? Is chaos its precondition? (1) Complete, in the form of war. (2) Partial, by way of growing unwillingness to assume responsibility. (3) And its reciprocal, unwillingness to yield authority—in government, in business, in education, trade unions, social agencies. Or will the chaos come about directly out of the breakdown of mechanization, whether because there are too few people to service it or because, increasingly, it is being made to break down in the interest of that well-known expanding economy.

One could go on but the issue is amply clear. Again in Mr. Mumford's paper, given at the conference on "Challenges to Democracy in the Next Decade," he expressed himself on essentially the same problem, " 'The System' saving labor to displace life," and "Exterminating mankind in the name of security." Admiral Rickover had a simple answer. "Our assignment," he said, "is not to let technology interfere with democracy any more than we let democracy interfere with technology." Mr. Sol M. Linowitz, chairman of the board of the Xerox Corporation, carried the argument a step further by proposing we find out how technology can enforce democracy!

127

Presiding over large enterprises and many men, as they do, board chairmen and admirals sometimes lose sight of the fact that there are situations not subject to their will or any man's. They would probably agree, for example, that one cannot have one's cake and eat it too; from there it might be possible to demonstrate that the law of contradiction holds in other situations as well; and that if we use up our energies with mechanisms, we find them unavailable for thought; that if we kill the spirit with bureaucracy, it will prove wanting for the preservation of freedom; that if an important part of the national income has to go into persuading people to buy what they don't want, or even what they do, correspondingly less will be left for education; that if we invest all our resourcefulness and drive in an expanding economy, we suffocate with "means, which we have, ends which we have lost from view, including that ultimate end, the human soul and what it needs for its own happiness and growth."

Analytically this is what we are talking about when we use those high-sounding expressions about "the wheels of progress." All part of the same conference, the chairman of McCann-Erickson Corporation International pointed out in more modish psychological language that advertisers, by showing people what is available to them, provide the incentive for work. If he believed there was a human soul, he forgot to mention whether

128

for its happiness and growth, it did better on television, a frigidaire, work, a motorcar, or some suitable combination of these. Was there a step to be taken beyond what he advertised? If so, he also forgot to mention it; this was someone else's advertising job.

Annually spent on advertising are about $7½ billion (1962), annually spent on defense more than $50 billion. These are largely nonproductive expenditures. Suppose, for example, we were to raise teachers' salaries with some small part of these funds? Or prolong the G.I. Bill of Rights instead of raising tuition in New York State University pursuant to the governor's idea for financing education? Or, with added numbers of the ethically and intellectually educated, implement the Alliance for Progress in Latin America? Or enlarge the Peace Corps in Asia and Africa? How would this look as a defense program? Or any other measures suggesting we still remembered we were human? Remembered that the motives with which we fight are at least as important as the weapons. Numberless psychological experiments have shown that the strength and the purposiveness of an action are directly correlated with the adequacy and the power of the motives that prompt it. Granted the far greater complexity, it would appear that the most critical moments in the World Wars went to the Allies not by force of arms but by reason of what they had to defend.

A similar inference suggests itself with reference to the American Revolution and the War of 1812. Briefly, since actions of whatever kind demand related motivation, it follows that bravery, endurance, life itself are fully and freely offered neither under compulsion nor yet to win Congressional Medals but to protect the freedom in which one shares because it is the core of what it means to be human. Only the untrammeled spirit attains to the summits.

Friendship is such a summit, embracing humanity—lacking humanity there is no friendship —spontaneous after we had emerged from the primordial struggle, and before we had perfected the man-made impasses; when, with no apologies, time might still be used "unorganized," personally for those things that mattered. Today they depend on conscious choice—can we afford them? Take time from work and from public relations— in business and education and politics? From trying to keep abreast of this culture and its unremitting acceleration, from endless meetings if we have a sense of the public purpose, from the hours that belong of right to the family and family responsibility, from the diversion that is essential, and the essential solitude?

To decide for genuine disinterested friendship amid these complexities arouses attention; most of us have felt we had to give it up. We gave it up without noticing it, gave it up so thoroughly we didn't even miss it until someone brought it back, after it had become a rarity, with something like the value of a rarity.

Although not all rarities necessarily have value: the crafts, for example, some of the most exquisite, have, when we have been lucky, left their products behind; of their skills not a trace. Conservation has limited meaning in relation to objects, little or none in relation to skills. Even the rare craftsman of today—I think of a man with a hand press, still providing a good living—feels he is obsolescent, if not obsolete, and that this is as it should be. One asks him why.

Briefly the costs are prohibitive. But then comes the next question, What are we paying for? Paying for beauty, workmanship, standards of excellence and achievement; compare the satisfactions both of buyers and of workers of these and other days. Is it inevitable that the bargain between past and future has in any area to be on an all-or-none basis? Can we not choose to take infinite pains for limited activities in limited amounts, and pay for them with what we save from built-in obsolescence, to name only one of the many areas of deliberate waste? Is it, in a word, anything but inertia that prevents deliberately choosing both from the past and the future?

This is the question of questions. To it the answer runs often, "I am an optimist." Twentieth-century expression of an eighteenth-century formula, "All for the best in the best of all possible worlds," thus reserving "judgment" until after the event. Is it pessimism to suggest that the pragmatic uses of judgment, if any, be before the event?

Or is it the higher optimism? The conviction that mankind, with increasing knowledge, may play not a decreasing but an increasing role in its own destiny as it competes for larger and higher stakes, negatively and positively.

11

YOUTH

The Climax Where There Has Been

No Dramatic Development

I visited Italy in 1935 when the Mussolini dictatorship was hardening. The elder Ruffini, in his seventies, and his son, in his early thirties, made an unforgettable contrast. Having refused the Fascist oath, the elder Ruffini had left the university and his Turin palace, to live at Borgofranco, where his ancestral country seat was in the throes of being made livable in the twentieth century. I couldn't help contrasting his son's paralyzing pessimism with his own resilient energy: "He has not lived long enough, he does not know that these things pass."

At times, for shorter or for longer periods, life's sordidness and its difficulties lie heavily on the young. They see themselves historically heir only to the misery of the ages, equally in the unrelieved gloom of the thoughtful and the devil-take-the-hindmost of the thoughtless.

In America their birthright of unrivaled material well-being, their privilege and prestige in virtue of being young, make for a climax where there has been no dramatic development; where, perforce, there can be none because youth is itself virtue, and age, if not vice, at least evil. So have we deprived them of hope.

Moreover, that sense of helplessness is pervading.

We feel ourselves, according to the mood, chessmen of muddle-headed governments that don't know the game, or jetsam to be cast up on God knows what shore by the tidal wave of history.

If one were to pick just one reason for this state of mind, it would be the short-range view of things; the closeup of life makes individual features loom so immensely large that it becomes impossible to look beyond them, vision is cut off, and the people perish. For truncated vision is rendered permanent by bureaucracy, which defines as cardinal sin any attempt to look beyond the particular subdivision in which one has been immured. Management then discovers to its amazement that junior executives at the magic moment of managerial decision are unwilling to enlarge their area of responsibility, and the result: training courses in residence at selected colleges and universities. But the effort to restore spiritual vitamins to life proves to be more complex than enriching our impoverished foods.

Recognizing only too well the incubus of the bureaucratic load, discussed in a previous chapter, one has nevertheless also to ask oneself, Could this cumulative sense of helplessness under which we are reeling while we are probably the only nation on this planet that could bring order out of chaos if we only knew how, could this sense of helplessness be somehow connected with our blind worship of youth, our identification with the young —not only with the very young for whom life is opening up as a uniformly exciting adventure without prejudice or discrimination, but with the young and the doctrinaire who have all the passion and prejudice and conviction and sophistication that come of knowing without having lived, the consciously, pridefully young who have neither earned their privileged position, nor justified it in terms of independence and courage—"outward and visible signs of an inward and invisible grace," the grace of genuine inner freedom before life's prejudices close in.

On one of those eternal days of early spring a small boy mounted the open deck of a Fifth Avenue bus of that period and shouted, responding to the open sky above him, "We're free! We're free!!"

Follow him down the inclined plane of the decade; had he still the enthusiasm to shout, what would it be? "We're secure! We're secure!" But he couldn't shout that, because in current terms there is no security.

A feverish quest for this, the holy grail of materialism, destroyed what we had of it. Overwhelming defense costs equally defy a labor or a business government to balance the budget in any real sense —in time, in effort, in any of the amenities of living. From education to soil conservation, community services suffer. And a citizenry, once independent, sees itself by singly imperceptible changes successively a band of explorers, revolutionaries, architects of the Republic, rugged individualists and captains of industry, chairmen of boards and presidents of labor unions, stockholders and jobholders—economic and political, members of street gangs and the prep school set, all "regular guys" whatever their role in life. At first creeping, then galloping conformism joins hands with security —political, economic, military—with anti-Communism, Daughters of the American Revolution, or other rubrics of the antisocial.

The regular guys suspect the irregulars of poaching, of taking their jobs or spoiling their fun; the academics with armies of regulars attack the moderns, usurping the spotlight; big business battles desperately for "normalcy" if it does not happen to want government to guarantee or reimburse losses; unions carve out their domains, foe is synonymous with nonmember. Come the loyalty probers, professional guardians of the national se-

136

curity—if less audible now, correspondingly more insidious as the renegades get their chance to be "regular." In the presence of a nation of witnesses only less scarred by silence than speech, the demagogues ride to hounds with the independents at bay. Again men kill the thing they love, for freedom alone is security.

Again René Dubos, studying the record, observes that each age produces its characteristic illness: smallpox, tuberculosis, polio were successively epidemic until medicine caught up with them; epidemic today are the diseases of tension, generating the universal quest for security, which in these terms can only be illusory. One way, perhaps in these days the only way, to security is courage, confidence sufficient to meet the demands the times impose. But in that case we should never have formulated the problem, never contracted these illnesses.

On the contrary, the deep-seated, not always conscious conviction of our inability to cope with major problems of our time feeds on itself. It motivates striking and compulsive preoccupation with a wide-ranging variety of contemporary phenomena, having in common only the ingenuity of devices employed to decrease the feeling of responsibility until it becomes commensurate with the supposed capacity—or incapacity—for thought and action.

Religion used to tell us that we should live for

the life to come—the reward not here but here-after—for which the terrestrial sojourn was long and continuous preparation. The religions born of today and today's perplexities enjoin us to live only for today, and with the divine guidance that each new day provides anew. We are successful to the extent that we can "empty" ourselves, empty ourselves both of vision and experience, potential obstacles to the directness, the clarity, the fullness of the inspiration we seek from above.

Pure chance, or limited aspirations and investments for success characterize a whole range of activities from bingo and quiz programs to jigsaw and crossword puzzles. "Never have so many spent so much time for so little."

Still another way of shrinking our world with every show of virtue is to leave things to the "experts," from science and law and public relations, to art and poetry and politics.

In short, we circumscribe our demands, and especially our responsibilities until they equal the modicum of confidence we still possess. Yet in the actual unlike the mathematical world minimum confidence cannot, "as we approach the limit, be smaller than any assignable quantity." Nature with its relentless drive toward self-preservation totals the reduced life aspirations, lets us know in our deepest unconscious that these fragments no longer make a whole, that security too has its law of diminishing returns and vanishes in the desperation to preserve it.

Youth is the season of the senses. Age passes through and beyond it, meets and survives the sorrows, the joys, and the boredom, lives once more in the young, reaches its values, when it is wise, in the course of long and varied experience of living. It is the task of the young, who are not too young, to help restore the continuity and the sense of life as a whole, learn that misery like love neither comes only once nor lasts forever.

How did helplessness, conformism, security become the creed of an America born of the love of freedom, and especially of American youth? Independence take the form of blind violence in the gangs, of trying out narcotics in the schools, or violating dormitory rules in the colleges? How did it, in short, become conforming aberration, standardized daring that leans and trades on the security supplied by the group. Basically, to be sure, the major responsibility must be lodged with the generations of parents and grandparents who pursued the usual and the obvious course of gravitating from one extreme to another: from excessive discipline to no discipline and excessive indulgence; from puritanical inculcation of duties to "having fun," not just as the highest but as the only goal; from the approved attitude of "speaking when spoken to," to center stage by virtue of being young; from this adulation of youth to its simultaneous betrayal: the wars to no purpose, the dying before having lived! That, felt the young, had to be prevented, *coûte qui coûte*, any experience was better than none. And if it shocked their elders, so much the better—the heirs to a shocking world would show they could outdo even the shocks of their heritage.

But the pendulum rhythm showed itself in the young as it did in their parents, and the compensatory spiritual swing began to appear. It needs to be carefully nurtured in this contemporary Babel in which dating begins at age twelve, in which schools and colleges depend increasingly on I.B.M. machines, and television supplements Westerns and murder mysteries with science fiction as lurid as it is commonplace.

The issues of *Life* and *Time* for July 5, 1963, are illustrative, with articles respectively on teen-agers crashing parties by Robert Wallace, and on the Peace Corps.

From the former: "If there is one thing the man is *not*, it is naïve. . . . Nonetheless he was startled when his daughter, age 15, said, 'Daddy, I think you'd better hire a policeman.' . . . But in the end he took his daughter's advice. . . . Gang party crashing by teen-agers, a phenomenon for almost a decade, has become a menace that frightens and confounds suburban parents and police alike. . . .

". . . Sweden, which has few slums and is also a thoroughgoing 'welfare' state, has one of the

140

highest rates of juvenile delinquency on earth. In Japan, where reverence for elders as established custom is immemorial, juveniles today commit 21% of the nation's crime vs. roughly 12% in the U.S. . . .

". . . Contemporary teen-agers speak of themselves as 'us' and of their elders as 'them.' Rightly or wrongly, many of them feel threatened and helpless in the world created and controlled by 'them.' They regard that world as a sorry mess and wonder why they should feel 'committed to it.' . . . To other teen-agers 'the acquisitive society,' typified in suburbia, seems pointless. What is the object, they ask, in accumulating material wealth, seemingly only for its own sake? . . .

". . . 'I'm not sore at anybody,' said the Westchester teen-ager who threw the beer can through the picture window. . . .

". . . 'In a . . . secular society,' writes Professor Toby, 'material goals are so prominent that it may be unbearable to have less income than one's neighbor.' . . .

" . . . What follows is the consensus of advice from more than a dozen police chiefs in the New York area, but it will doubtless be valid in suburban communities anywhere in the nation:

"Do not mingle socially [parents] with teen-agers at a party—you are a square, a bore and a spy——but by all means make your presence felt. . . .

"For large parties—25 or more—hire an off-duty policeman. . . .

"If you have taken none of these precautions and find yourself confronted with drunken and truculent guests or crashers, do not try to handle them forcibly. Run, do not walk, to the nearest telephone and call the police.

". . . [The crashers'] question, 'Where's the party?' can be ominous or pathetic. For what answer is the suburban teen-ager truly searching? Where, in all the boredom and pressure of his world, *is* the party?"

And from "The Peace Corps" in *Time:* "Said Shriver in his Congressional Message: . . . 'To sum up: while the Peace Corps may not be as good as its reputation, it is almost as good as its intentions.'

"That sounds just about right to the U.S. and to many other countries. Hearing about the work of the Peace Corpsmen, one country after another has asked to be included in the program. Where Peace Corpsmen have already been sent, requests have come in for more. Even Nkrumah's Ghana, where government-run, Communist-lining newspapers still rail at the Peace Corpsmen as 'agents of the U.S. Central Intelligence Agency,' the government itself has urgently requested that the 113-man Peace Corps contingent be doubled. In Nigeria, where poor Margery Michelmore caused all that commotion, the present group of 297 teachers is being increased, at Nigerian request, to more than 600. Says a top official of the Nigerian Ministry of Education: 'There is not one of the various foreign aid schemes working in this country that can beat the Peace Corps.'

". . . Such has been the history of the Peace Corps that it has inspired, in the two short years of its existence, no fewer than twelve other nations, to try to follow suit. They are: Argentina, Belgium, El Salvador, France, Great Britain, Honduras, Italy, Japan, New Zealand, Norway, The Netherlands and West Germany."

Each of the ages of man contributes to a total which we shall never see nor understand in terms of any one age. If we lose the sense of the whole, we feel cornered in our particular sector, with the possibilities easily exhausted except for the no-holds-barred, last desperate effort of self-preservation; and we may, indeed we will, be deceived even in this, should it become our single aim.

In rare moments of "maturity," in the moments of search and of silence, we know with profound inner certainty that except we invite the final one, the day of the wars must be ended—not just the wars of the nations and the ideologies, but the wars of the classes and the animosities of the generations. Is it the vastness of the summons to close ranks on both sides in one upward struggle, that makes it inaudible, leaves it unrecognized? That summons to a second salvation, without a Messiah —the summons to humanity to save itself.

143

12

AGE AND DEATH

Humanity for Its Fulfillment Needs Life

Limited and Open-ended, Mortal and Immortal

—for Pressure toward Accomplishment,

for Boundless Possibility

The phenomenon is well-known of the telescoped view of his own life seen by a drowning man in an instant of time—extreme illustration of what is achieved under pressure. This is the meaning of death for life.

To most of us it becomes tangibly evident only as life's limit approaches. For youth the lifespan is a period in which one has not in any definite way to reckon with time: we put something off, confident, or hopeful, or just assuming that we will come to it "later." Until one day it becomes suddenly and pitilessly clear that many of the things we wanted to do we shall never do, and that our most important account is with time. It is measured now in specific accomplishment—what "the books" have to show of debit and credit for a life on earth.

Simultaneously we may be able to use time less advantageously because age is often less controlled, less purposeful in its actions, less in command of its reactions; because, externally, the social and the functional structures built in the course of the decades—and which for a time vastly extend individual range—begin to lose their supporting columns as other lives end or their capacities diminish. These supports, so long taken for granted, have now to be replaced with varying degrees of difficulty and effectiveness, or may prove irreplaceable.

As one becomes critically aware of time both absolutely and operationally, the latter end of life feels called upon not only to make its own personal reckoning but to extract and refine coin of the future from the accumulated capital of experience. This again is a moment of conversion of the material and the finite into the spiritual and the unending, the endlessly transmitted. To have won a moment of human existence against infinite odds—to have lived the color and the tedium, the struggles, the bliss, and the occasional peace, the failures and the triumphs—constitutes, in thinking

145

and feeling a moral urge, a kind of promissory note to increase purpose, understanding, wisdom, to reduce futility, circumstance, ineptitude.

This is the psychology and the philosophy of later life when age fulfills its mission as today it does with greater and growing incidence. It rises to challenge a contradictory culture which boasts of unprecedented prolongation of life yet looks even upon later middle age as a drag on any and every activity which an employer has in his giving, whether professional, technical, administrative. And notwithstanding the record in their latest score of years of such as Robert Frost, Learned Hand, Albert Schweitzer, and such others, known to smaller circles, as Lillian Gilbreth, Carl Buhler, Stephen P. Jewett, and the many uncounted and unknown. Neither has comparable age been a bar to higher political office from President, Prime Minister or Supreme Court Justice, to Governor, Senator, or Cabinet Minister. The attempt appears never to have been made to find a conversion formula between the creativity, energy, impatience of youth and the experience, wisdom, endurance of age.

Basically, profoundly, we understand only our own experience, and in that sense death remains forever beyond us, but pondering it increasingly as we approach it, suggests some relevant considerations.

It has been said that what goes living into a

146

dwelling place remains even when life in the accepted sense has gone out. And this appears to be true as well on the cosmic stage. The life of Israel of more than fifty centuries ago breathed life into contemporary Israel; it was at this late date probably the single most potent factor in creating a community and a nation.

In what sense then are our Jewish forebears lifeless, in what sense alive in Israel?

We find there the ancient and the contemporary intimately and inevitably interrelated as a magnet to iron filings—the metaphors are interchangeable. To be there is to grasp why Jews could be resettled nowhere save in Palestine if it was even partially open to them. For this rugged pioneering effort needed more than persecution to motivate it. Home had remained home down the generations as a promised land again fulfilled its promise and became the potent factor for unity among Jews of thirty-five nations and cultures worlds apart: in a new age of isolation by exclusion, it took the world's castaways to its bosom, and transmuted into strength the ages of suffering. It gave dignity and the sense of ongoing destiny to the handicapped, the hunted, the unwanted, as it did to active and successful protagonists of the world's struggle to be moral and rational and free.

Yet another area of our early cultural inheritance suffuses with a sense of fulfillment today's beholder of the Parthenon—a sense of origins and goals, of root and branch. It reaches down into unexplored strength, and up into limitless aspiration, complete, without being final—"recognized at once as part of the world's inheritance," *as which it has remained.

Site planning and architecture, art and literature of ancient Greece emanate today, as then, profound and confident understanding "of what human life and what the human mind is for."† This is instinctive, immediate conviction as one touches land on the peninsula. The stream of spiritual life is felt to be as irresistibly continuous as of physical life—not so of individual consciousness with which at times one tends to identify it. As one tries to get clear just how one relates to the past and the future, to fathom the meaning to us of death and of life and of the continuity of each with the other, it is borne in on us that individual life is both limited and open-ended. Open to what has gone before and what comes after, reshaping both and being reshaped, endlessly; rooting and branching, growing at both ends, dying at both ends—fruitfully or fruitlessly.

Humanity for its fulfillment needs to be both mortal and immortal, time-borne and eternal—for pressure toward accomplishment, for boundless possibility. These are the short- and the long-range motives, mainsprings of action that combine the

---

* W. A. Wigram, *Hellenic Travel.*
† H. D. F. Kitto, *The Greeks.*

frontier with the infinite worlds beyond, the measured with the measureless.

This is the way of spiritual evolution in which
only the instantaneous is lived once. We continue
to live and we live again, both what has been and
what will be. Neither is entirely open to us, nor
ever completely closed. Discovery is only of what
has always been, and freedom, life itself, may be
checked or enhanced equally by visions of the future or memories of the past. These are so inextricably the stuff of consciousness that they tend to
make of continuity immortality as an almost inevitable psychological extrapolation.

In this ultimate attempt to understand, the problems of faith enmeshed in life are confronted head-
on to dominate death. Faith takes many different
forms, but fundamentally three: it may be faith in
one's fellow man; in the ultimate outcome of the
work of one's hand or brain; which means an ordered universe and, basically, an ordering source
or principle, in which one may also believe directly. "Whoever plants a seed beneath the sod,
and waits to see it push away the clod, he trusts
in God."

We are all planting seeds, and waiting to see
them push away clods. Some are prepared to wait
longer, with aspirations extending beyond themselves, like the head gardener in the Alpinum of
Vienna's Belvedere, contributing, he said, "only
one or two stones to the creative work of more

149

than a century; this is our St. Stephen's Dome."
His co-workers were his predecessors and his suc-
cessors and the gardeners of all the world's alpi-
nums exchanging the seeds of six continents.

The scientist or the philosopher who hopes that
his hypothesis will fit the universe around him is
predicating a continuing, advancing order, discovered and undiscovered, enlarged, in time even
reconceived, with which he may somehow collaborate. The nature of the questions he puts and
the methods of seeking answers are what account
for getting them or failing to get them, ultimately
for making the universe increasingly intelligible,
increasingly responsive—even if we gravitate at
one time toward the simpler, at another toward
the more complicated, at times even the apparently
contradictory.

The man who has found his niche in life is
therefore essentially a happy man, a man of faith,
not necessarily religious in any usual sense. But he
is at once believer and creator; nor could he be
either without the other. This is faith in its most
general aspect, a precondition of human life.

How does it become religious in the narrower
sense? A specific instance:

The postwar, as usual, brought a wave of religion. In the psychosomatic era it followed the
trend: go through the forms, it said, meaning will
come.

I did.

150

I shared my concern for a very sick friend with a new and ardent convert. She said she would pray for him. "But the closer the pray-er to him for whom the prayer, the nearer a favorable result."

"Even if prayer seems to me supererogatory in the scheme of a just, all-knowing God?"

"Even so."

Then I learned by personal experience what the mental hygienists have known for a long time: that tolerance is very low for engaging in what is meaningless—either one desists from action or one endows it with meaning.

I started with the only prayer I knew, the Lord's Prayer. In a few days what had been words became symbols intellectually and morally charged, gradually with passion.

What happened? Proselytizing had failed in my case. The literature I had been given was for those who already believed. This was an experience to challenge the unbeliever, and I needed on my own account to analyze, to understand. Putting it generally, form had taken on substance, substance emotion, emotion faith. Faith had become fortitude. This was the background of search for the meaning of meaning.

I became acutely aware in the process of the extent to which in our time and our country words have largely lost their meaning. They are subject today to a degree of inflation compared with which prices look moderate; they are overused in print, in type, in speech. Advertisers vie with advertisers, broadcasters with broadcasters, and each with the other. The epithets they employ swell like balloons with no limiting factor of tensile strength. Writers with a real regard for language attempt to make it over. Educators advise, "Avoid using it if you possibly can."

What about us—ordinary men and women with a profession? Not only do we constantly see and hear practically without awareness, but we talk that way too. Words and phrases, rhythm and slang come without thinking, go without meaning. A kind of treadmill culture seems to exact superficial response to each and every pressure, even when, as often as not, the pressures cancel out, like the coinciding crest and trough of advancing waves from different centers.

But, rightly used, words are the single form of expression that we have in common to convey the intricacies of meaning; they are the channel to ourselves and our universe and each other. Time is needed to use them rightly, and also tranquillity. And when we have no tranquillity, neither do we have time in any sense that counts.

Our culture has conspired to take both. Its tendency to make us spectators, or even less, while the work of the world is done by specialists (of whom we may even be one) and propagated by machines, gives us a thinner and thinner surface on which to skate through the motions of living.

152

We become more and more abstractly critical of events with which we have no contact and for which we feel little or no responsibility. The large mass of us have become the kind of epiphenomenon without whom business as usual, pleasure as usual, life would go on—as usual.

Or not quite. The mechanism runs faster and faster. And the word? The thought? The search for meaning? These tend to disappear as words are devalued. We begin to fear, some of us—many unhappily do not—a life used up in trivia, a runaway machine that presently will come to grief. "Can we stop it?" we ask in sudden consternation.

First, we must get back time. Time for words to have meaning, above all meaning for ourselves. It may be we know this as prayer. And it may be the ancient, far-seeing Wisdom enjoined us to pray lest thought perish—disinterested thought, nonspecialized thought, thought at its most essential—and the search for meaning.

Words in this sense are the balance wheel of mankind, or its lightning rod. In the vast area of the universe humanity functions well within a very limited range: the eye, for example, sees only a minute part of the spectrum in the wave lengths from gamma to radio; and absolute zero is not much more congenial to the living state than boiling heat.

Morally, spiritually, we are probably in the same case, as Aristotle discovered long ago. That we can take only a limited amount of frustration all of us know. But since we are not as a rule equally cursed with success, we are less conscious of the fact that we can bear even less of it before it degenerates into callousness, love of power and other less recognizable forms of destruction. Prayer, words with one's deeper self, with God, or Life, or Love, or Spirit, absorbs what is excessive in misery or good fortune. It brings home to us all those myriad conspiring factors in our successes and our failures that are independent of our contriving in any ordinary sense. We have a share in them only as we know them, we command them only as we acknowledge them.

The circle closes: do they derive from chance or from an ordering source? Just posing the question makes the leap to religion, and to attempt the answer raises yet another question, "How could we collaborate with chance?" as we do with a world order when we are sufficiently disciplined.

The positive answer, positing a controlling moral intelligence and will, surmounts too the all but insurmountable—reconcilement with individual death in somewhat different versions of ongoing life, the doctrines of reincarnation and of immortality. For imagination falters, confronting the subjective silence of our own curiosity, the closing shears on the thread of our own creativity.

Can we then so far identify ourselves with the stream of life and history as to find fulfillment and tranquillity in knowing ourselves part of "one in-creasing purpose" . . . "through the ages," make the other personalities interwoven with our own, so integrally part of our deepest selves that they continue to evolve beyond the time of their physi-cal presence as we carry them with us in our own evolution? As we will, in turn, be carried by others.

Immortality in this sense demands mortality—as the Greeks pronounced no man happy until he was dead, so is every other estimate of an unfin-ished existence impossible, in its accomplishment or in its conduct, as life or as art. . . .

Death may become magnetic when it is con-ceived to perpetuate happiness or end despair. At times, and in less extreme situations, it has prob-ably beckoned all of us from an infinitely weary-ing world to the peace of a shaded greensward.

EPILOGUE

The point of view here presented is characterized by some as romantic, by some as conservative—characterizations that "simplify" complex situations with overused, therefore partially meaningless terms. Both miss what is essential, viz., to guard against a basic human weakness, the nearly irresistible tendency toward excess in a given direction; for once to anticipate humanity's recurring days of reckoning, inherent in extremes of whatever kind. That we do not even try, notwithstanding the gravest distress signals, points to one of the deepest of contradictions in the contemporary outlook, and to an almost suicidal abrogation of collective responsibility.

Shall we attribute to coincidence, to "corporate responsibility," to unconscious historical analogy, or to all of these, the production legends of two recent motion pictures with Roman themes? Alistair Cooke writes of *Cleopatra* in the *Manchester Guardian Weekly* of June 20, 1963:

"Cleopatra barged into New York last night on her poop of beaten gold, and 10,000 New Yorkers on the streets outside yearned to be with her.

"That is the only proper measure of the biggest,

loudest, shiniest, heaviest (600 lb. per print) most rainbow-hued film in history, which was originally budgeted for $1,200,000 and has a single desperate purpose, to recover the $42 millions it actually cost. [On the basis of these figures, what happened in the course of production can be better imagined than described.] . . .

"Consequently, all the half-way celebrities with names to hawk were invited to abide by a time-table which would bring their faces and voices to the breathless millions on television. A banker who took 200 seats was asked to invite not so much the most beloved of his personal friends as the company presidents, big-time lawyers, cereal and mattress tycoons who might do the film 'most good.' . . .

"The financial chivalry of New York was in the audience and was visibly stunned by a pageant that seemed less like a motion picture than a nine-ring circus and fashion show. . . .

"Even the *New York Times* surrendered to 'a brilliant, moving, and satisfying film . . . a surpassing entertainment, one of the great epic films of our day.' . . .

" 'At best,' concluded another critic, 'a major disappointment, at worst an extravagant exercise in tedium.' "

In the production of *Ben-Hur* I give as typical only a few stark facts about the galley. The most painstaking research went into the blueprints which were then submitted to an engineer. He pronounced them excellent except for the fact that the galley would overturn. Obviously, they said, this was impossible, the research procedures had been too thorough to permit such a contingency. Construction followed according to plan. The galley was duly floated with great acclaim; then it overturned.

But too much was at stake to permit discarding the galley. That left the alternative of an artificial lake with water of such density that it would sustain the galley's upright position. The "water" formula was submitted to the engineer. He gave the direst warnings against using one of the chemicals. Again the warnings were ignored with the result that the lake became solid almost immediately. In brief, the general method of Lamb's roast pig continued to be followed throughout the staging of the film.

We see ourselves the vanguard of the West, the civilization of change and individualism; contrasted with the static East, submerging the individual in the larger human groups, if not in the human sea. Yet, the creed we live is not change except as we equate it with its direct antithesis, momentum.

Change is what breaks momentum. Rarely do we risk it voluntarily.

"The unexamined life is not worth living." But

just this is what we *are* living, nearly exclusively. The unexamined life is predominantly the young life. And the young, as we have seen, are as well our idols as our gods. The very young cleave with their strength, in any predicament, to the patterns they know, profoundly frightened of change. It takes years to undermine that illusion of safety. And conformism passes from physical to spiritual, to the undeviating mores of adolescence and post-adolescence, back later to the materialism of status and middle age.

Awareness develops only very gradually of the place and the value of tolerance. It comes with age and experience, not only tolerance but tolerance of change. Insight into its necessity: one has known in the span of time how the future became the past. Hence the effort to influence it, sensibly if one can: for to exchange given unsatisfactory situations for their precise opposites, as we are prone to do, holds little or no promise of bringing us nearer to the good life.

Rummaging through papers of some thirty years ago, I chanced upon the forgotten slogan "What we need is a dictator," that formula of impotence from Harding-Hoover-Mussolini days, expressing cumulative discontent with years of vacillation in the Presidency. "Where will he come from?" had asked the professor of mathematics. "Will he ride in on horseback, or will I be the dictator?"

The "reasoning" prompting the slogan must have run somewhat as follows: "We cannot live with Hoover; therefore we cannot live with democracy; therefore we need a dictator." And the supporting evidence, "Mussolini made the trains run on time!" Is there anything that savors more of prehistory? Not the prehistory of fact but of fancy?

Reasoned change is basic to the idea of progress. It depends on insight, wisdom, stamina. These traits tend to be reinforced by age or disaster. A query suggests itself: is it in part our thinking of age too as disaster that in some of us prompts new resistance and enterprise in later life? The disparaging view of age as useless and the positive implications of youth as dynamic have produced a variety of results: have hidden in some of our "senior citizens," have dammed in others that confluence of widely distributed sources of individual experience, which in the long-lived, developed personality may become the flow of reasoned change, of considered reintegration of people, circumstances, events. The distinctive cast of the West, unknown to ourselves, has been given to an appreciable degree by men and women who have lived longer and lived consciously.

Quoting from other writers has one of its important justifications in the superior formulations they may have found for thinking related to one's own. In *The Undirected Society*, Sir Geoffrey

Vickers underscores once again the more striking gaps, excrescences and contradictions of our time: ". . . the feeling is widespread that what cannot be objectivized is at least suspect." This is one of the century's great obsessions, objectivity accelerating to impersonality; it was spawned in the hallowed procedures of scientific research. ". . . the passionate concern of our age, especially in North America, with what is called the 'conquest' of outer space [is] a preoccupation which is not explained, though it may be financed, by concern for defense. I can imagine that some historian in a future age may find summarized in this concern the essential weakness of our own. Why, he may ask, when its inner space, socially and individually, was so manifestly unexplored and unreclaimed, did our age spend so vast a share of our human and material resources on exploring the barren void outside the atmosphere? Was it not, he may answer, that here was the only remaining field in which man could remain aloof from his subject matter, a still non-participant observer?

"[Yet] the understanding which comes from scientific analysis would be an equivocal, if not a sinister force, if it ceased to be attendant on the understanding which springs from compassion."

As in fact it has ceased, for compassion itself is presumed to lead astray in this world of objectivity and principle, causes and ideologies.

On the working class level, too, fragmented factory jobs limit, more often destroy the workers' horizon. Small wonder they have no use for leisure except further isolation, absorbed each in his own television or portable radio; reaching his home by express highways, with pace, exits, stops, prescribed, continuingly subordinated to the well-being of his machine: "Don't drive if you tend to be emotional," runs the advice of the Metropolitan Life Insurance Company.

To date no advice has been offered for disposing of nerves and emotions in the West Side Bus Terminal, in which one succumbs to the sheer horror of automated efficiency without automated passengers. Surrounded by microphones that explain with relentless insistence just where the hundreds of buses are going, a sense of helplessness builds up to desperation. As far as the eye can see or the soul can pierce, nothing and no one human is available for assistance. A *New York Times* reporter wrote on June 29, 1963:

"More than 35,000 persons swarmed into the sweltering terminal between 5 and 6 P.M. According to one bus company employe, it was 'a mess.'

"Children screamed and wept, elderly women pushed through the terminal with heavy valises and ticket buyers waited in lines 15 to 20 persons deep.

" 'It's impossible and inadequate,' said one observer, adding that travelers must usually arrive at least one hour before their bus departs.

162

"Other complaints include poor information facilities, a shortage of red caps and inadequate signs."

Some of the newer airports follow suit. Luggage does everything save carry its owner. Far and wide, however, there is none to carry the luggage.

Mr. Vickers speaks of new needs. ". . . the need for a change of course, reflecting a changed sense of what matters most and redistributing the energies of society in accordance with this change of emphasis."

The emphasis changes, to be sure, but not because it "reflects a changed *sense* of what matters." The sense of what matters abides, timeless. Change inheres in the finite, the timebound, the evolving. And the sense of what matters may be satisfied in one situation by what has been called romantic, in another by the classical; in one by the conservative, in another by the radical. If the sense of what matters is fixed as it is by human nature, while that same sense must operate in time and therefore in change, it is the *content* of what matters that is bound to vary appropriately.

"Deliberations such as we have had [in this research into Canadian industrial development], affect action," Sir Geoffrey continues, "not so much by answering present questions as by releasing into the stream of decision-making the consciousness of changed need [changed not subjectively but objectively], which in turn moulds the decisions of the future. The greatest step in answering new questions is to ask them."

It follows from the foregoing that the end of a culture is at hand when one ceases to ask them, when momentum carries everything before it. ". . . the great depression of the thirties brought home to all that relief is no substitute for employment and thus revealed the social significance of work." To whom? And with what result?

The struggle continues for fewer and fewer hours while the free time gets to be more and more of a bore or becomes the means to earn more money in second jobs or in overtime. Until, as of now, the electrician in a well-known museum earns more than the curator in far fewer hours.

These signs of a decaying culture are all about us, and just beginning to be noticed. Not enough, however, so that the new questions are being asked, asked seriously, insistently.

"Freedom is the condition in which we can *set and revise* the governors by which we live. It does not give us a course; it gives us only one of the conditions for our unending search for our course. When freedom is denied, it becomes a goal; but when it is possessed, it is only a beginning." The beginning of what, is our decision. Are we waiving that most fundamental of all rights, to which destruction is the only alternative, by bestowing on momentum the label of progress?

A moving paragraph from Albert Schweitzer's autobiography may constitute a kind of closing exhortation to the human confraternity not to abandon to fear and fatigue the struggle of the ages for the Use of Reason:

"I am pessimistic in my judgment of humanity's present position. I cannot talk myself into its being any less bad than it appears to be. On the contrary I am aware of our being on a road which will lead us, if we travel it further, into a new kind of Middle Ages. I am aware in its full magnitude of the spiritual and material misery to which mankind is surrendering through forgoing thought and the ideals to which it gives rise. Nevertheless I remain optimistic. I have retained belief in truth as an inalienable childhood faith. I am confident that the spirit of truth is stronger than the power of circumstance. To my mind humanity can have no other fate than what it itself prepares through its own attitude of mind [*Gesinnung*]. I do not believe therefore that it must go the way of destruction to the end. . . .

"Because I trust in the power of truth and the spirit, I believe in the future of mankind." (Translated from *Aus meinem Leben und Denken* for the *New School Bulletin*, October 16, 1950.)

CLARA W. MAYER

Clara W. Mayer was born in New York City in 1895. After graduation from Barnard College in 1915, she did graduate work at Columbia University from 1915 to 1919. She received a Doctor of Letters degree from the New School for Social Research in 1948.

Miss Mayer's association with the New School goes back to its beginning in 1919 when she was a student there. She became a trustee of the school in 1924, and was secretary to its board of trustees from 1931 to 1946. She served the school as a vice-president from 1950 to 1962. Her successive positions as an administrator of the New School also include being the assistant director from 1931 to 1936, associate director from 1937 to 1943, dean of the school of philosophy and liberal arts from 1943 to 1960, and dean of the school from 1960 to 1962.

Miss Mayer is a member of the American Anthropological Association, the American Folklore Society and the American Ethnological Society.